Quality of Life in Asia

Volume 24

This series, the first of its kind, examines both the objective and subjective dimensions of life quality in Asia, especially East Asia. It unravels and compares the contours, dynamics and patterns of building nations by offering innovative works that discuss basic and applied research and emphasizing inter- and multi-disciplinary approaches to the various domains of life quality. The series appeals to a variety of fields in humanities, social sciences and other professional disciplines. Asia is the largest, most populous continent on Earth, and it is home to the world's most dynamic region, East Asia. In the past three decades, East Asia has been the most successful region in the world in expanding its economies and integrating them into the global economy, offering lessons on how poor countries, even with limited natural resources, can achieve rapid economic development. Yet while scholars and policymakers have focused on why East Asia has prospered, little has been written on how its economic expansion has affected the quality of life of its citizens. This series publish several volumes a year, either single or multiple-authored monographs or collections of essays.

Shoirakhon Nurdinova

Happiness and Life Satisfaction in Central Asia

Springer

Shoirakhon Nurdinova
Kimyo International University in Tashkent
Tashkent, Uzbekistan

ISSN 2211-0550 ISSN 2211-0569 (electronic)
Quality of Life in Asia
ISBN 978-981-95-3081-6 ISBN 978-981-95-3082-3 (eBook)
https://doi.org/10.1007/978-981-95-3082-3

This Springer imprint is published by the registered company Springer Nature Singapore Pte Ltd.
The registered company address is: 152 Beach Road, #21-01/04 Gateway East, Singapore 189721, Singapore

Preface

Synoptic Outline

This book approaches the life satisfaction and happiness of Central Asian people from an empirical perspective. It examines the current trend of subjective well-being in Central Asia over time. The book examines happiness and the relationship between economic and noneconomic factors using econometric models. Issues related to gender, culture, and social norms are examined to provide a wide range of results. This book is a groundbreaking effort to reveal the intricate structure of quality of life and well-being in Central Asia. It serves as a valuable resource for scholars and policymakers focused on happiness-oriented development in the region. Additionally, it holds significance for researchers exploring the relationship between well-being and the various factors that influence it.

Tashkent, Uzbekistan

Shoirakhon Nurdinova

Competing Interests The author has no competing interests to declare that are relevant to the content of this manuscript.

Introduction

Happiness and life satisfaction are central themes in the study of human well-being, encompassing a wide range of factors that influence how individuals perceive and experience their lives. In Central Asia, these perceptions are deeply intertwined with local cultural, economic, political, and social contexts. This book investigates the complex interplay between these factors and happiness in Central Asia, exploring how theoretical perspectives, economic conditions, political environments, and social norms shape subjective well-being in the region. Each chapter provides a distinct lens through which to understand these dynamics, offering insights into the multifaceted nature of happiness in this diverse area. The book explores the complex interplay between these factors and happiness in Central Asia, drawing on data from the World Values Survey (WVS) to provide a comprehensive understanding of subjective well-being in the region. Chapters investigate a different aspect of this interplay, offering insights into how various dimensions contribute to happiness in Central Asia.

Chapter 1 sets the stage by providing a comprehensive overview of theoretical perspectives on happiness and life satisfaction, particularly as they apply to Central Asia. This chapter reviews relevant literature, highlighting various models and theories that explain the factors contributing to happiness. It includes a discussion of local efforts and contemporary have approaches emerged in response to the region's unique challenges and opportunities.

Central Asian societies are characterized by their rich cultural traditions and historical experiences, which play a crucial role in shaping individual and collective well-being. Understanding how these theoretical perspectives apply to the region requires an examination of both global frameworks and localized adaptations. The chapter covers a range of theories from positive psychology to cultural dimensions of well-being, providing a foundation for analyzing happiness in the context of Central Asia's sociocultural landscape. In addition to theoretical insights, this chapter also identifies gaps in the existing literature and suggests future research directions. By focusing on both applied and theoretical perspectives, it aims to offer a holistic understanding of happiness in Central Asia, setting the stage for a deeper exploration of the region's unique challenges and opportunities.

Chapter 2 examines the multidimensional factors influencing quality of life (QoL) in Central Asia. It focuses on economic, medical, environmental, and sociocultural dimensions. The countries, Kazakhstan, Kyrgyzstan, Tajikistan, Turkmenistan, and Uzbekistan, have different development challenges from post-Soviet transitions, resource dependency, and climate vulnerabilities. By analyzing key indicators such as healthcare access, economy, and environmental degradation, this chapter provides a comprehensive assessment of well-being disparities across the region.

Chapter 3 shifts focus to the intersection of economics and happiness, examining how economic indicators and conditions influence subjective well-being in Central Asia. This chapter explores both historical and contemporary perspectives, analyzing how economic development, poverty, inequality, and employment impact happiness in the region.

Historically, Central Asia has experienced significant economic transformations, from Soviet-era central planning to post-independence market reforms. These economic shifts have had profound effects on individuals' lives, influencing their perceptions of well-being and satisfaction. By reviewing historical data and contemporary trends, Chap. 3 provides insights into how economic changes have shaped happiness in the region. The chapter also considers how economic indicators such as GDP, unemployment rates, and income inequality correlate with subjective well-being. It examines the relationship between economic growth and happiness, noting that while economic development can lead to improvements in quality of life, it can also exacerbate disparities and create new challenges. This analysis emphasizes the importance of considering both economic and noneconomic factors in understanding happiness.

Chapter 4 explores the relationship between political indicators and happiness, focusing on how political environments and governance structures impact subjective well-being in Central Asia. This chapter reviews existing literature on political stability, freedom of choice, and political participation, highlighting how these factors influence happiness in the region.

Central Asia is marked by a variety of political regimes, from authoritarian governments to emerging democracies. This diversity provides a unique opportunity to examine how different political contexts affect well-being. The chapter considers how political stability, freedom of expression, and political engagement contribute to or detract from happiness. A key aspect of this analysis is the exploration of freedom of choice as a political factor influencing happiness. In more restrictive political environments, individuals may experience limitations on their personal freedoms, which can impact their overall well-being. Conversely, greater political freedom and participation can enhance individuals' sense of autonomy and satisfaction. By reviewing literature on these topics, Chap. 4 aims to provide a nuanced understanding of how political factors shape happiness in Central Asia.

Chapter 5 examines the impact of social norms on the well-being of individuals, organizations, and societies in Central Asia. This chapter focuses on how traditional social norms, particularly those related to family dynamics and gender roles, influence subjective well-being in the region. Central Asia is characterized by strong collectivist values and patriarchal structures, where traditional family roles and gender expectations play a significant role in shaping individuals' experiences. Women, for example, are often responsible for household chores, childcare, and elder care, which can have profound implications for their well-being and life satisfaction. The chapter explores how these social norms impact various aspects of life, including personal fulfillment, social support, and community engagement. It also considers how changes in social norms, such as increased gender equality or evolving family structures, may affect happiness in the region. By analyzing the interplay between social norms and well-being, Chap. 5 aims to provide a comprehensive understanding of how cultural and societal expectations shape individuals' experiences of happiness in Central Asia.

This book offers a multidimensional exploration of happiness and subjective well-being in Central Asia, integrating theoretical, economic, political, and social perspectives. Each chapter contributes to a deeper understanding of how various factors intersect to influence well-being in this diverse region. By examining theoretical models, economic conditions, political environments, and social norms, the book aims to provide valuable insights into the complex dynamics of happiness in Central Asia.

Understanding happiness in Central Asia requires a nuanced approach that considers the region's unique cultural, historical, and political contexts. This book seeks to illuminate these complexities and offer a comprehensive analysis of how various factors impact well-being in the region. Through this exploration, it aims to contribute to the broader discourse on happiness and provide a foundation for future research and policy development in Central Asia.

Contents

1 Quality of Life in Central Asia: Contemporary Approaches 1
1.1 Introduction 1
1.1.1 General Information About Uzbekistan 6
1.1.2 Happiness in Uzbekistan 9
1.1.3 General Information About Kazakhstan 11
1.1.4 Happiness Level in Kazakhstan 12
1.1.5 General Information About Kyrgyzstan 14
1.1.6 Happiness in Kyrgyzstan 15
1.1.7 General Information About Tajikistan 17
1.1.8 General Information About Turkmenistan 18
1.1.9 Happiness in Turkmenistan 20
1.2 Conclusion 21
References 22

2 Quality of Life Issues in Central Asia 25
2.1 Introduction 25
2.1.1 Economic Challenges and Opportunities 26
2.1.2 Cultural and Social Dimensions 27
2.1.3 Environmental and Climate Issues 28
2.1.4 Healthcare and Access to Medical Services 29
2.2 Conclusion 30
References 31

3 Happiness and Economics in Central Asia 33
3.1 Introduction 33
3.1.1 Economic Development and Happiness in Kazakhstan 34
3.2 Economic Instability and Subjective Well-Being in Kyrgyzstan 40
3.2.1 Economic Factors of Happiness in Tajikistan 44
3.2.2 Income and Life Satisfaction in Uzbekistan 48
3.3 Conclusion 52
References 54

4 Happiness from a Political Perspective in Central Asia 61
4.1 Introduction 61
4.2 Governance and Subjective Well-Being in Kazakhstan 62
4.3 Revolution, Political Situation, and Happiness in Kyrgyzstan 67
4.4 Political Freedom and Happiness in Tajikistan 72
4.5 The New Government of Uzbekistan and Happiness 76
4.6 Conclusion 81
References 82

5 Happiness and Social Norms in Central Asia 89
5.1 Introduction 89
5.2 National Identity and Happiness in Kazakhstan 90
5.3 Values and Life Satisfaction in Kyrgyzstan 98
5.4 Gender Norms and Happiness in Tajikistan 102
5.5 Social Capital and Life Satisfaction in Uzbekistan 106
5.6 Discussion 112
5.7 Conclusion 114
References 119

Chapter 1
Quality of Life in Central Asia: Contemporary Approaches

Abstract This chapter explores the concepts of happiness and life satisfaction in the unique sociocultural context of Central Asia. It investigates the historical, religious, and societal factors that influence the perception and pursuit of happiness in the region. Additionally, it examines the impacts of modernization, globalization, and socioeconomic changes on the well-being and life satisfaction of individuals in Central Asia. Furthermore, the chapter provides insights into the role of family, community, and traditional values in shaping the subjective well-being of Central Asian populations. By drawing on empirical studies and theoretical frameworks, this chapter aims to offer a comprehensive understanding of happiness and life satisfaction in Central Asia and highlights areas for further research and intervention.

Keywords Central Asia · Happiness · Life satisfaction · Well-being · Globalization

1.1 Introduction

Central Asia, consisting of Kazakhstan, Kyrgyzstan, Turkmenistan, Tajikistan, and Uzbekistan, shares commonalities in religion, culture, history, and language, fostering regional cooperation on various issues such as transportation, security, border concerns, and environmental challenges (Batsaikhan & Dabrowski, 2017). Following the dissolution of the Soviet Union in 1991, Central Asia underwent a significant transformation from centrally planned to market-oriented economies, leading to diverse development paths among the countries. This transition has had varying impacts on living standards, employment, and social structures, necessitating a nuanced examination of economic growth and its distribution to understand its influence on happiness (Naghdi et al., 2021). Countries like Kazakhstan and Turkmenistan, endowed with abundant energy resources, have experienced substantial economic growth, while nations like Kyrgyzstan and Tajikistan, lacking such resources, face challenges in achieving sustainable development (Spechler, 2008).

S. Nurdinova, *Happiness and Life Satisfaction in Central Asia*, Quality of Life in Asia 24, https://doi.org/10.1007/978-981-95-3082-3_1

Tajikistan endured a civil war until the mid-1990s, Kyrgyzstan grappled with political instability, and Kazakhstan emerged as an upper-middle-income country with political stability. The economic landscape of Central Asia has been shaped by these historical contexts, influencing the region's trajectory over the past few decades. The region's economic performance has been extensively analyzed, with studies focusing on factors such as total factor productivity, energy intensity, and economic growth patterns (Li et al., 2019). Additionally, the nexus between agriculture, water, energy, and environmental degradation in Central Asia has been empirically examined, highlighting the interconnectedness of these sectors in the region. Furthermore, the impact of urban sprawl on the development of cities in Central Asia has been a subject of study, reflecting the evolving urban landscapes in the region. Despite the shared history and cultural ties, Central Asian countries have pursued distinct economic paths, leading to disparities in development outcomes. The involvement of external actors like China and India in the region has added another layer of complexity to Central Asia's geopolitical and economic dynamics (Laruelle et al., 2010). Understanding the economic challenges and opportunities in Central Asia is crucial for formulating policies that promote sustainable development, address regional disparities, and enhance overall well-being in the diverse countries of the region.

Kazakhstan is the only country that has achieved the "Very high Human Development" category, whereas other Central Asian countries are in the "high" or "medium" Human Development categories (UNDP, 2024). As a result, the quality of life in Central Asia varies across countries.

Despite numerous studies on Central Asia, more research on subjective well-being is needed to provide an in-depth explanation (Inoguchi & Fujii, 2012). As quality of life studies are overlooked in regions, few research studies are conducted by local researchers. Some research has been conducted on the impact of public sector employment and financial satisfaction in Central Asia on subjective well-being (Demircioglu & Sharipova, 2023; Sharipova & Kudebayeva, 2023a). Kudebayeva and her colleagues (2022) performed a comparative analysis of social capital and subjective well-being over time in Kazakhstan, Uzbekistan, and Kyrgyzstan. Omarova and Kenzhakimov (2023) reported that Central Asian countries have a relatively low level of public satisfaction with their quality of life, according to the index of happiness.

The quality of life in Central Asia is seen as multidimensional, incorporating subjective well-being, living standards, housing issues, and various satisfactions in different life domains (Kim, 2023). The happiness function includes life satisfaction, feelings of happiness, and subjective health perceptions. His analysis results show that Tajikistan has the highest subjective well-being value of 9.14, despite having the lowest level of economic development. Uzbekistan has a subjective well-being value of 9.10, indicating a high level of well-being. Moreover, Kazakhstan, which has relatively high levels of economic development among Central Asian countries, has subjective well-being value of 7.87. Kyrgyzstan with 7.09 indicated the lowest levels of well-being in the region. In Kazakhstan and Kyrgyzstan, rural residents are happier and more satisfied with their lives than their urban counterparts are. In terms of urban settings, the findings demonstrate that capital city residents have the lowest levels of happiness and satisfaction with life in Kyrgyzstan. In contrast, in Kazakhstan, regional center dwellers have the lowest levels of happiness and life satisfaction. This is explained by the varying socioeconomic development of the capital cities and regional centers in the two countries (Makulbayeva et al., 2023).

Fewer surveys have been conducted on happiness in Central Asian countries than in developed countries. The Gallup poll includes positive emotions, including happiness, enjoyment, and laughter, and three negative emotions, including anxiety, sadness, and anger, in Central Asia. The life evaluation measure used in the poll is the Cantril Ladder, a zero- to ten-point response to the following question: "On which step of the ladder would you say you personally feel you stand at this time?". Using life evaluation data, the World Happiness Report estimates happiness trends worldwide.

Table 1.1 shows the level of happiness in Central Asian countries. Even though there are some fluctuations in trends, the overall happiness level from 2006–2022 increased in Central Asia (Fig. 1.1).

Table 1.1 Happy life years in Central Asia 2010–2019

Rank	Nation	Satisfaction with life	Life expectancy in years	Happy life years
103	Tajikistan	5.8	67.4	39.1
87	Turkmenistan	6.4	69.8	44.5
82	Kazakhstan	6.6	70.6	46.9
54	Kyrgyzstan	7.4	70.4	52.3
34	Uzbekistan	7.7	73.6	56.3

Source R. Veenhoven, Rank report Happy Life Years in Nations 2010–2019, World Database of Happiness

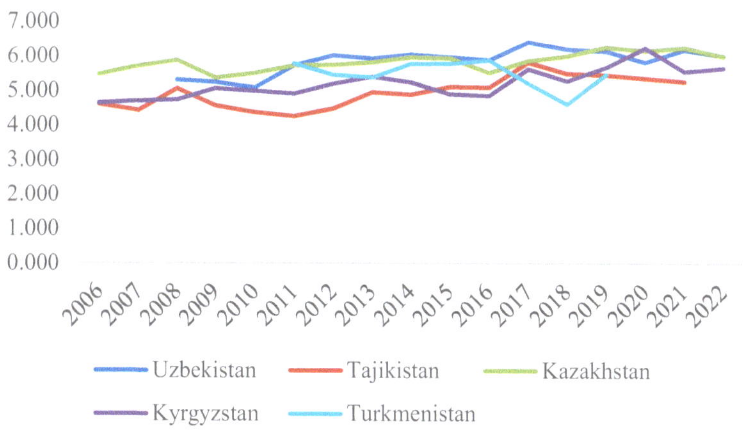

Fig. 1.1 Happiness in Central Asian countries. *Source* World Happiness Report (2022)

The Happy Life Years (HLY) metric, which integrates subjective life satisfaction with objective life expectancy, provides valuable insights into quality of life variations across Central Asia from 2010 to 2019. The data reveal several noteworthy patterns that challenge conventional development paradigms. Uzbekistan emerges as a regional leader in well-being (56.3 HLY), outperforming wealthier Kazakhstan (46.9 HLY) through a combination of high life satisfaction (7.7) and relatively strong life expectancy (73.6 years), suggesting the importance of social cohesion and gradual reforms in sustaining well-being independent of GDP. Kyrgyzstan demonstrates a similar paradox, achieving higher life satisfaction (7.4) than its economic position would predict, potentially attributable to robust informal support networks. Conversely, Kazakhstan's underperformance relative to its economic stature indicates possible governance-related well-being deficits, while Tajikistan's low HLY (39.1) reflects the compounded effects of economic fragility and social disruption from labor migration. Turkmenistan's mid-range performance (44.5 HLY) in an authoritarian context raises questions about the relationship between political systems and well-being measurement.

The table examines inequality in happiness across Central Asian nations, measured through the standard deviation of life satisfaction scores on 0–10 scales from multiple surveys. The findings reveal significant cross-national variation in happiness dispersion, suggesting differing levels of social cohesion and equitable well-being distribution in the region.

Turkmenistan demonstrates the lowest happiness inequality (SD = 1.93) among Central Asian states, potentially reflecting either strong social homogeneity or suppression of dissatisfaction in an authoritarian context. Tajikistan follows closely (SD = 1.97), possibly indicating shared hardship in one of the region's poorest nations. Uzbekistan shows moderate dispersion (SD = 2.07), which may relate to its combination of gradual economic reforms and persistent traditional social structures. Kazakhstan (SD = 2.35) and particularly Kyrgyzstan (SD = 2.47) exhibit greater happiness inequality, potentially reflecting: 1) more pronounced urban–rural divides, 2) higher economic stratification, or 3) greater freedom to express dissatisfaction in relatively open political climates (Table 1.2).

The relatively low inequality in more authoritarian states (Turkmenistan, Tajikistan) versus higher inequality in more open societies (Kyrgyzstan) suggests a potential trade-off between political freedom and happiness homogeneity. The findings

Table 1.2 Rank report inequality of happiness in nations 2010–2019

Rank	Nation	Standard deviation of 0–10 life satisfaction	Number of surveys
17	Turkmenistan	1.93	9
21	Tajikistan	1.97	10
33	Uzbekistan	2.07	1
95	Kazakhstan	2.35	2
114	Kyrgyzstan	2.47	2

Source R. Veenhoven, World Database of Happiness

partially challenge conventional inequality theories, as the poorest nation (Tajikistan) shows lower happiness dispersion than wealthier Kazakhstan.

The table examines the comparative levels of happiness across Central Asian nations as measured by self-reported life satisfaction scores (0–10 scale) from multiple surveys conducted between 2010–2019. The data reveal a clear hierarchy of national happiness levels that challenges conventional economic development narratives.

Uzbekistan emerges as the regional leader in average happiness (7.7), significantly outperforming its neighbors despite having a lower GDP per capita than Kazakhstan. This finding suggests the importance of noneconomic factors such as social cohesion (e.g., traditional mahalla systems) and gradual economic reforms in sustaining high levels of subjective well-being. Kyrgyzstan follows closely (7.4), reinforcing the observed pattern that less wealthy nations can achieve relatively high happiness levels, potentially through strong community networks and cultural resilience.

The data present two notable anomalies. First, Kazakhstan ranks only third (6.6) despite being the region's economic powerhouse, indicating a potential "happiness paradox" where resource wealth does not automatically translate to greater life satisfaction. Second, Turkmenistan's mid-range score (6.4) in an authoritarian context raises questions about measurement validity versus genuine social stability mechanisms. Tajikistan anchors the bottom of the regional rankings (5.8) (Table 1.3).

The analysis examines the relative positioning of Central Asian nations in global happiness rankings, comparing their life satisfaction scores (0–10 scale) with Western counterparts. The data reveal several noteworthy patterns that challenge conventional development narratives while highlighting unique regional characteristics. Uzbekistan (7.7) and Kyrgyzstan (7.4) report life satisfaction scores that not only surpass those of several Western European countries—such as Belgium (7.5), the UK (7.4), and Germany (7.4)—but also equal or exceed those of the United States (7.0), France (6.8), and Japan (6.2). This phenomenon suggests a paradoxical relationship between GDP per capita and subjective well-being, potentially attributed to robust traditional social structures, such as mahallas and community networks, which serve as significant buffers against economic hardship. Cultural values may further prioritize alternative determinants of happiness beyond material wealth, while the post-Soviet transition appears to have preserved psychosocial support. In contrast, Kazakhstan (6.6) demonstrates lower life satisfaction despite its higher economic development, scoring

Table 1.3 Average happiness in Central Asia 2010–2019

Rank	Nation	(0–10) life satisfaction	Number of surveys
14	Uzbekistan	7.7	1
24	Kyrgyzstan	7.4	2
67	Kazakhstan	6.6	3
78	Turkmenistan	6.4	9
103	Tajikistan	5.8	10

Source R. Veenhoven, World Database of Happiness

beneath its less wealthy regional peers and comparable petrostates like Qatar and the UAE. This anomaly may reflect factors such as the resource curse's impact on social cohesion, the disruptive effects of rapid urbanization on traditional supports, and governance quality issues that are not captured by economic indicators. Additionally, the examination of Western Europe reveals substantial variation in happiness levels, with Nordic countries at the forefront (Denmark 8.2, Finland 8.0) and Southern Europe lagging significantly (Greece 6.0, Portugal 6.1), indicating that welfare state models and cultural factors play critical roles in mediating the relationship between wealth and happiness. The divergent outcomes observed in authoritarian contexts, exemplified by Turkmenistan (6.4) outperforming Russia (5.9) and Belarus (5.9), while Tajikistan (5.8) remains at the regional low, further emphasize the intricate interplay of social systems and individual well-being.

Another indicator is the measure of happiness, which is based on whether an individual smiled and laughed yesterday, is a subjective indicator of well-being. While this measure may not capture the full spectrum of an individual's happiness and life satisfaction, it can provide insights into their immediate emotional state and overall positivity. Gallup's data on whether an individual smiled and laughed yesterday provide insight into the happiness or positive emotional experiences reported by individuals across different regions and over time.

Figure 1.2 shows whether an individual smiled and laughed yesterday in Central Asia. In 2006, 63% of people in Uzbekistan, 60% in Kazakhstan, 63% in Kyrgyzstan, and 49% in Tajikistan reported laughing or smiling a lot the previous day. These indicators were below average globally, which was 71% in 2006. From 2006–2023, there seems to be some variation, but generally, there is an increasing trend in the percentage of Central Asian people reporting that they smiled or laughed many times the day before. Particularly noticeable increases occurred in Uzbekistan, Tajikistan and Kyrgyzstan, whereas decreases occurred in Turkmenistan (from 65% in 2009 to 52% in 2019). Throughout most years, the percentage for Kazakhstan tends to be lower than the global average, which ranged from 55 to 68% during the years provided.

Happiness varies widely across Central Asian countries due to a combination of cultural, economic, and social factors unique to each nation. Uzbekistan has seen improvements in various socioeconomic indicators. However, challenges such as unemployment, income inequality, and limited political freedom can influence happiness levels.

1.1.1 General Information About Uzbekistan

Uzbekistan, officially known as the Republic of Uzbekistan, is a landlocked country located in Central Asia. Uzbekistan shares borders with Kazakhstan to the north, Kyrgyzstan to the northeast, Tajikistan to the southeast, Afghanistan to the south, and Turkmenistan to the southwest (Fig. 1.3).

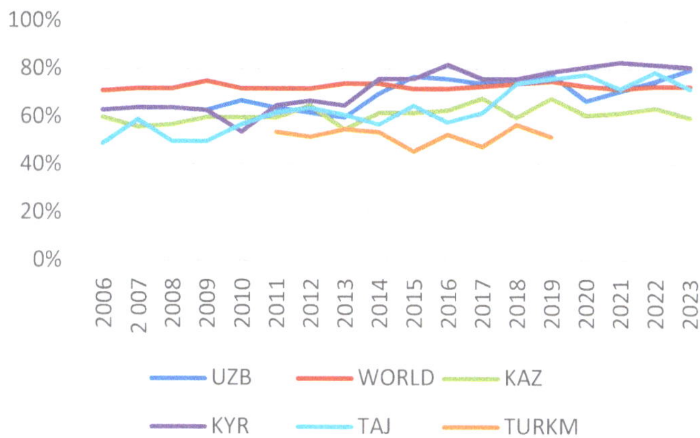

Fig. 1.2 Positive emotions in Central Asian Countries. *Source* Gallup Poll (2024)

Fig. 1.3 Map of Uzbekistan

The Uzbekistan population reached 37 million in 2024, and Uzbekistan is the most populous country in Central Asia. The gender demographics of Uzbekistan indicate a slightly lower proportion of females (49,7%) in the population. The population density of Uzbekistan in 2024 is approximately 82.29–86 people per square kilometer.

Uzbekistan has a diverse population distribution, with both rural and urban areas playing significant roles in shaping the country's demographics. According to the National Statistics Agency of Uzbekistan, the rural population in Uzbekistan accounted for approximately 49% of the total population in 2024 (Demografiya, 2024). The distribution of the population between rural and urban areas has significant implications for various aspects of life in Uzbekistan. For example, the distribution of birth rates tends to be greater (27) in rural areas than in urban areas (25.9). There is a noticeable difference in life expectancy between urban and rural areas. Urban regions (75.1 years) generally have higher life expectancies than do rural areas (74.1 years). This discrepancy is attributed to several factors, including access

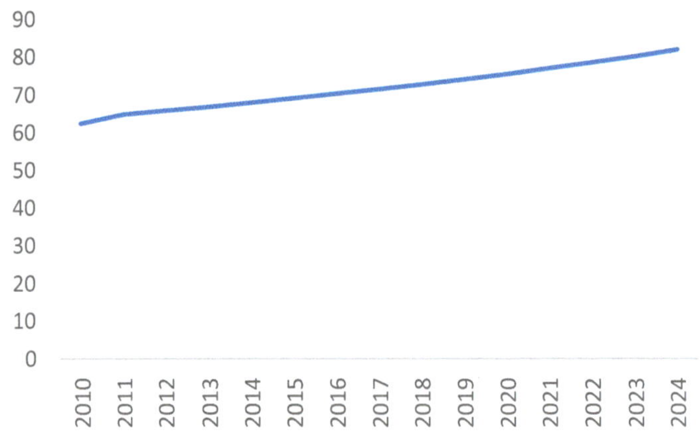

Fig. 1.4 Population density in Uzbekistan, 2010–2024. *Source* Statistical agency of Uzbekistan (2024)

to higher-quality medical care and better workplace safety in urban areas. Specifically, Tashkent, the capital city, has the highest life expectancy in Uzbekistan, with an average of 77.1 years, which is notably above the national average.

This figure represents a relatively stable population density over recent years. The population density in Uzbekistan has shown a gradual increase from 62.4 people per square kilometer in 2010 to 82 people per square kilometer in 2024 (see Fig. 1.4). The country's total land area is approximately 447,000 square kilometers.

The infant mortality rate for Uzbekistan in 2023 was 8.5 deaths per 1000 live births, with a 0.2% decline from the previous year. This rate has been decreasing over the years, indicating positive progress in reducing infant mortality. The mortality rate among children under five years of age was 9 in rural areas, whereas it was 15.6 in urban areas in 2023. The prevalence of multidimensional poverty is notably higher in rural areas, at 23.2%, than in urban areas, at 13.9% (Uzbekistan Multidimensional Poverty Index Report, 2023).

Uzbekistan is a diverse and multicultural country with more than 130 various nationalities and ethnic groups. Uzbeks are the most common people in Uzbekistan, followed by Karakalpaks, Tajiks, Kazakhs, Kyrgyzs, and Russians. While international migration from Uzbekistan was based on the movement of nontitular nations to the homeland, after the 2000s, the influx of labor migration increased to Russia, Kazakhstan, South Korea, Türkiye, etc. (Kamp & Nurdinova, 2022).

Uzbekistan ranked 106th out of 193 countries and territories worldwide in the Human Development Index (HDI) report. As of 2022, the HDI score for Uzbekistan has slightly increased to 0.727, which was the highest observation since 1990. This places Uzbekistan in the category of countries with high levels of development, as scores over 0.700 are considered to indicate such high levels (UNDP, 2024).

The literacy rate in Uzbekistan is quite high at approximately 99.5%. The gross national income per capita was 8,204. USD (PPP) in 2021 (World Bank Open Data,

2024.). Approximately 4.2 million adults, accounting for 18.4% of the adult population, face multidimensional poverty, as they encounter deprivations in at least 34% of the weighted indicators (Uzbekistan Multidimensional Poverty Index Report, 2023).

1.1.2 Happiness in Uzbekistan

According to a recent world happiness report, Uzbekistan ranks 47th out of 143 countries. Uzbekistan's happiness level changed 0.97 points from 2006–2010 to 2021–2023. In the World Happiness Report (2022), which assesses happiness on the basis of factors such as GDP per capita, social support, life expectancy, freedom to make life choices, generosity, and perceptions of corruption, Uzbekistan has shown some improvements in recent years. The country's efforts to improve living standards, healthcare, education, and infrastructure could be positively reflected in its happiness ranking.

While the world happiness report evaluates current happiness, Gallup Poll has another emotional indicator related to the future that indicates how optimistic people are. The respondents are asked to rate life satisfaction over five years on a scale from 0–10 on the basis of current trends and personal aspirations. Figure 1.5 represents the percentage of respondents who rated their future life satisfaction as 7 or higher on a hypothetical ladder scale ranging from 0–10.

There are noticeable increases in some years (2010–2015), suggesting periods of perception of improvement in future happiness or life satisfaction.

The Happy Planet Index (HPI) measures how well nations are doing at achieving sustainable well-being. It is the closest to the top score registered in Vanuatu, with the Central African Republic having the worst well-being score (13.7), according to the happy planet index in 2021. Uzbekistan was ranked 44th out of 147 countries in the Happy Planet Index (HPI) for 2021. The HPI measures well-being and environmental

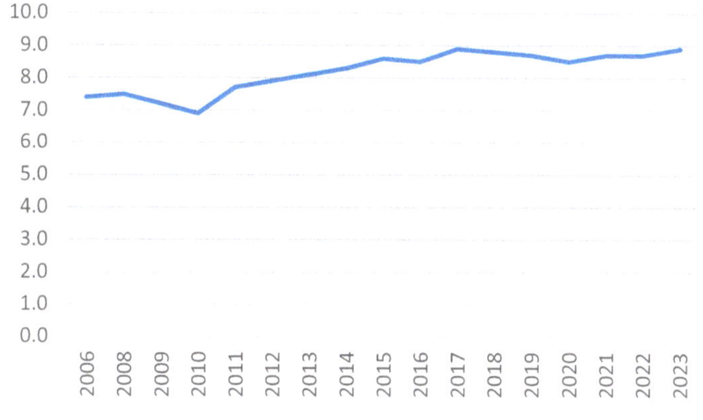

Fig. 1.5 Life Satisfaction over Five Years in Uzbekistan. *Source* Gallup Poll (2024)

Table 1.4 Uzbekistan's HPI scores

Year	HPI	HPI rank
2006	33,15	
2007	33,80	73
2008	33,89	69
2009	34,16	72
2010	33,99	77
2011	38,48	59
2012	40,43	48
2013	39,88	58
2014	40,69	55
2015	40,50	58
2016	40,22	60
2017	44,08	42
2018	42,65	50
2019	42,69	50
2020	40,63	66
2021	43,01	44

Source Happy Planet Index (2022)

sustainability, taking into account factors such as life expectancy, experienced well-being (happiness), and the ecological footprint. Specifically, Uzbekistan's score on the Happy Planet Index for 2021 was 43.0. Table 1.4 shows that Uzbekistan's HPI scores have varied over the years, ranging from 33.15 in 2006 to 43.01 in 2021.

From 2006–2012, Uzbekistan's HPI scores gradually increased from 33.15–40.43, suggesting improvements in well-being and life expectancy and possibly a reduced ecological footprint relative to those of other countries. Uzbekistan's HPI rank has also fluctuated over the years, ranging from 42nd in 2017 to 77th in 2010.

Uzbekistan's mean happiness score of 7.7 suggests relatively high well-being, placing it near the top globally and the highest in its region. Uniquely, being male is negatively correlated with happiness in Uzbekistan, contrasting with many Western contexts where males tend to report higher happiness. The overall high happiness levels amidst lower GDP per capita suggest that noneconomic cultural factors and social trust might play more prominent roles, which is also observed in some non-Western studies. These differences highlight the importance of cultural context in understanding happiness, as some relationships evident in Western studies do not directly transfer to Uzbekistan (Nurdinova, 2024).

1.1.3 General Information About Kazakhstan

Kazakhstan is the country that is most economically developed in Central Asia. Kazakhstan has abundant natural resources, including oil, natural gas, and minerals. It has developed rapidly since gaining independence, with a focus on diversifying its economy beyond extractive industries into agriculture, manufacturing, and services (Fig. 1.6).

The GDP per capita reached from 7,554 USD dollars (PPP) in 1991 to 39,335 USD dollars in 2023. In the most recent Human Development Report by the United Nations Development Program (UNDP), Kazakhstan ranked 67th out of 193 countries and territories globally. This places Kazakhstan in the category of countries with a high level of human development. The life expectancy at birth in Kazakhstan is approximately 69.5 years. (UNDP, 2024) However, the National Statics of Kazakhstan shows different indicators for life expectancy, with values of 75.73 years for urban areas and 74.02 years for rural areas (Statistics Kazakhstan, 2023). Kazakhstan is one of the most urbanized countries in Central Asia, with a large proportion of the population, approximately 62.5%, residing in urban areas (Statistics Kazakhstan, 2024).

As of 2024, Kazakhstan has approximately 9.8 million males and 10.3 million females, with females constituting approximately 51.2% of the total population. The internal migration within the country has notably increased by 27.5%. Specifically, three regions Astana had 50,078 people, followed by Almaty and Shymkent (Fig. 1.7).

Kazakhstan is the only country that is categorized as receiving migrants in Central Asia. Country's *Oralman* project called Kazakhs to migrate to the historical motherland (A. C. Diener, 2005). Kazakhstan's population includes Kazakhs (the largest ethnic group), Russians, Uzbeks, Ukrainians, etc. The fertility rate in Kazakhstan

Fig. 1.6 Map of Kazakhstan

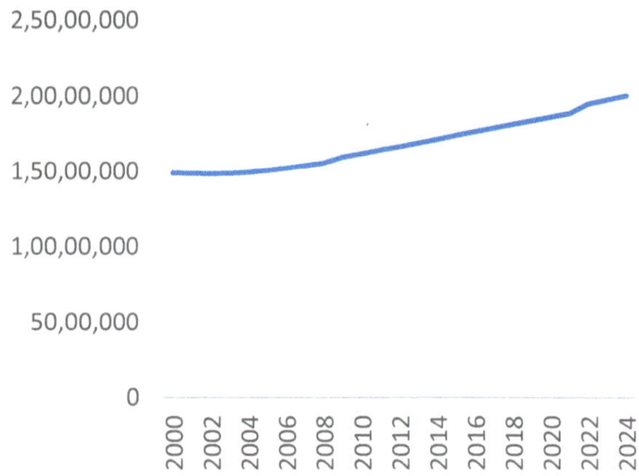

Fig. 1.7 Populations of Kazakhstan, 2000–2024. *Source* Bureau of National Statistics of Kazakhstan (2024)

decreased from 20.28 people (per 1000 people) in 2022 to 19.5 people in 2023. Infant mortality decreased from 18,82 (per 1000 live births) in 2000 to 7.68 in 2022. The rural infant mortality rate (8,41) was slightly higher than the urban infant mortality rate (7.2)(Statistics Kazakhstan, 2024).

1.1.4 Happiness Level in Kazakhstan

As the wealthiest and most developed country in Central Asia, Kazakhstan generally enjoys higher standards of living than its neighbors do. Economic growth and stability contribute positively to overall happiness levels, although urban–rural disparities and issues such as corruption can affect perceptions.

Figure 1.8 provided appears to represent life evaluation in five years scores for Kazakhstan across different years. These scores are typically based on surveys where individuals rate their life satisfaction on a scale, often ranging from 0–10. From 2006–2013, Kazakhstan's life evaluation scores showed a relatively stable range between 7.0 and 7.8, with some fluctuations from year to year. From 2014–2020, there was an overall upward trend, with scores ranging from 7.5–8.2 in 2020, indicating improved life satisfaction during this period.

The World Values Survey (WVS) includes questions related to happiness and subjective well-being among its extensive range of inquiries about societal values, attitudes, and beliefs. The survey is conducted across various countries and aims to capture cross-cultural differences and similarities in people's perceptions and experiences. The WVS includes questions for Kazakh people to rate their overall happiness. Figure 1.9 presents the responses to a survey question about levels of happiness in Kazakhstan.

A total of 28.7% of the respondents in Kazakhstan reported being very happy. A total of 55.8% of the respondents indicated that they were quite happy. This further suggests that a majority of the population feels positive about their happiness level,

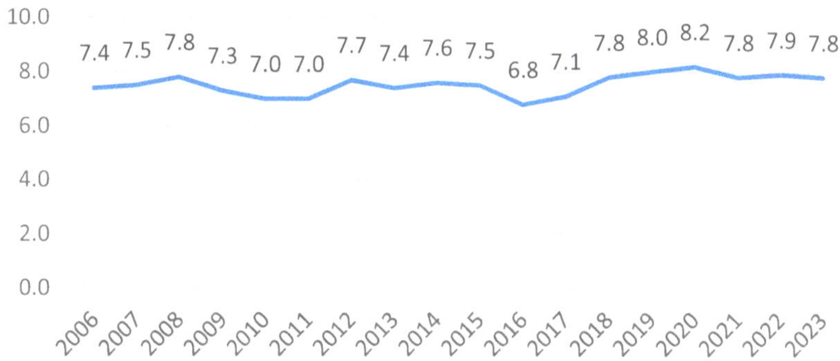

Fig. 1.8 Life satisfaction over five years in Kazakhstan. *Source* Gallup Poll (2024)

Fig. 1.9 Happiness level in Kazakhstan. *Source* World Values Survey Wave 7 (2022)

although to a slightly lesser extent than those who are very happy. A total of 10% and 0.5% of respondents reported being not very happy and not at all happy, respectively.

The table represents the Happy Planet Index (HPI) for Kazakhstan from 2006–2021 (Table 1.5).

The HPI score ranged from a low of 23.84 in 2006 to a peak of 29.88 in 2019. In 2021, the HPI score for Kazakhstan was 29.38. Kazakhstan's HPI rank has varied between 96th (in 2008) and 117th (in 2019), with a rank of 112th in 2021. From 2006–2011, Kazakhstan's HPIs gradually increased from the mid-20 s to approximately 29, indicating improvements in well-being and possibly more efficient use of ecological resources during this period. Later, the HPIs decreased slightly, reflecting potential challenges in maintaining or improving sustainable well-being. Since 2017, scores have stabilized around the high 20 s, showing consistency in sustainable well-being measures despite minor fluctuations.

Kazakhstan's average happiness score is 6.6 (on a 0–10 scale), placing it in the mid-range globally. While happiness levels generally increased during the 2010s, notable declines occurred in 2009 and 2016, with possible explanations discussed in the text. A distinctive feature of well-being in Kazakhstan is the disparity between cognitive satisfaction (low) and emotional well-being (relatively high), a pattern common among post-Soviet developing nations. Happiness inequality, measured by standard deviation, is moderately high, aligning with Kazakhstan's mid-tier global ranking. Additionally, the determinants of happiness in Kazakhstan diverge

Table 1.5 Happy Planet Indices (HPIs) for Kazakhstan

	HPI	HPI Rank
2006	23,84	
2007	24,60	102
2008	26,50	96
2009	25,21	106
2010	26,98	104
2011	29,27	104
2012	28,01	110
2013	27,72	110
2014	28,04	115
2015	26,53	120
2016	25,61	124
2017	27,29	122
2018	28,20	120
2019	29,88	117
2020	29,62	119
2021	29,38	112

Source Happy Planet Index (2022)

from those in developed countries, instead reflecting trends typical of post-Soviet developing economies (Jamanbalayeva & Tlenchiyeva, 2024).

1.1.5 General Information About Kyrgyzstan

Kyrgyzstan, officially known as the Kyrgyz Republic, is a landlocked country located in Central Asia (Fig. 1.10).

Kyrgyzstan has approximately 3.5 million males, constituting approximately 49.5% of the total population. The GNI per capita in Kyrgyzstan has fluctuated

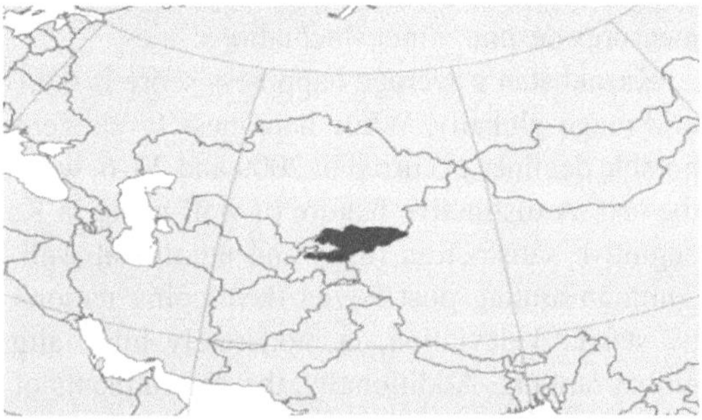

Fig. 1.10 Map of Kyrgyzstan

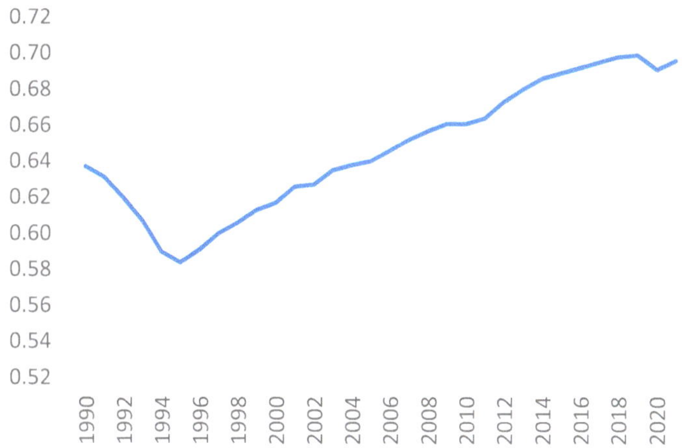

Fig. 1.11 HDI for Kyrgyzstan. *Source* UNDP human development index data (2024)

over time: from 4,624 USD dollars in 2010 to 5,823 USD dollars in 2022. The GNI per capita peaked in 2018 at 5,908 USD dollars (World Bank Open Data, 2024). Kyrgyzstan's territory is approximately 199,900 sq km, including several Uzbek enclaves in Kyrgyzstan (Megoran, 2010). Kyrgyzstan ranked as 117th out of 193 countries in the Human Development Index (HDI) report, with a score of 0. 701 (Fig. 1.11).

The majority of the population is ethnic Kyrgyz, with significant minorities of Uzbeks and Russians. The country has experienced political transitions and reforms since independence (Collins & Gambrel, 2017).

1.1.6 Happiness in Kyrgyzstan

This country has experienced political instability at times, impacting its economic development and overall well-being. Despite these challenges, Kyrgyzstanis often presents strong community ties and cultural resilience, which can contribute to a sense of happiness and belonging.

On the basis of the provided data on life satisfaction scores for Kyrgyzstan over the years, the figure shows life over five years. Kyrgyzstan's life satisfaction scores over five years have shown a generally increasing trend from 2006–2023, with fluctuations: the scores have varied from a low of 6.4 in 2008 to a peak of 8.6 in 2020. In recent years, relatively high and stable scores have been reported, indicating a period of perceived high life satisfaction (Fig. 1.12).

The table shows Happy Planet Index (HPI) data for Kyrgyzstan from 2006–2021. From 2006–2010, Kyrgyzstan's HPI scores gradually increased from the mid-30 s to approximately 38.20 in 2010, indicating improvements in well-being and possibly more efficient use of ecological resources during this period. From 2011–2015, the

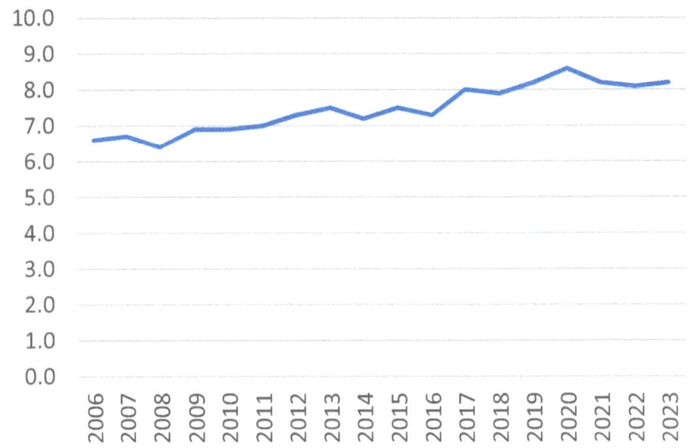

Fig. 1.12 Life over five years in Kyrgyzstan. *Source* Gallup poll (2024)

HPIs fluctuated slightly, with scores varying between the mid-30 s and the low 40 s, reflecting changes in environmental impact and life satisfaction measures. From 2016 to 2021, the scores show more significant variations, with a notable increase to 46.39 in 2020, followed by a decrease to 41.38 in 2021, suggesting fluctuations in sustainable well-being and ecological balance (Table 1.6).

Table 1.6 Happy Planet Indices (HPIs) for Kyrgyzstan

	HPI	HPI Rank
2006	34,71	
2007	36,61	62
2008	36,64	57
2009	37,79	61
2010	38,20	57
2011	37,30	66
2012	38,71	59
2013	40,22	55
2014	39,55	62
2015	37,26	76
2016	37,82	73
2017	43,91	44
2018	40,82	62
2019	43,09	48
2020	46,39	37
2021	41,38	53

Source Happy Planet Index (2022)

Kyrgyzstan's HPI rank ranged from 37th (in 2020) to 76th (in 2015), with a rank of 53rd in 2021. The HPI score ranged from a low of 34.71 in 2006 to a peak of 46.39 in 2020. In 2021, the HPI score for Kyrgyzstan was 41.38.

1.1.7 General Information About Tajikistan

Tajikistan is the only country that does not speak Turkish in Central Asia. Tajikistan has a population of 10.3 million people according to recent estimates (Fig. 1.13).

Tajikistan represents 126 out of the 193 countries with a score of 0.679, which is related to the medium development country category ("Analytical tables—Agency on statistics under the President of the Republic of Tajikistan", 2023). Life expectancy was 76.3 years in Tajikistan, 74.8 years for men and 77.9 years for women in 2022("Analytical tables—Agency on statistics under the President of the Republic of Tajikistan", 2023). The urbanization rate is quite low in Tajikistan, with approximately 28.8% of people living in urban places. The territory of Tajikistan is 143,100 sq km, and the population density was 71.3 in 2022.

Tajikistan is the most remittance-dependent country in Central Asia. Remittance receipts as a percentage of GDP were highest in Tajikistan and the Kyrgyz Republic among regional economies, amounting to 51% and 31%, respectively ("Migration and Development Brief 38 | KNOMAD," 2023).

Fig. 1.13 Map of Tajikistan

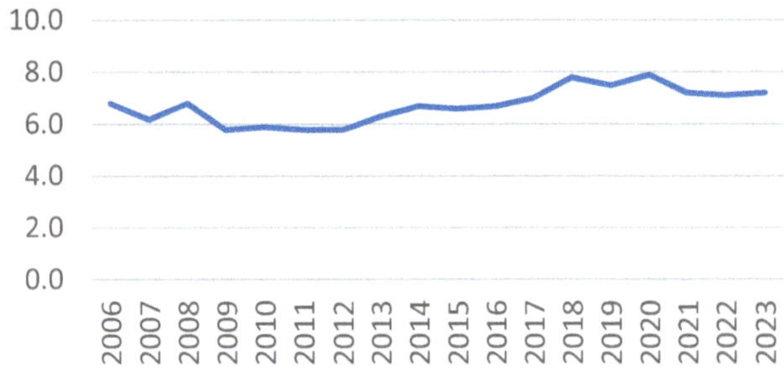

Fig. 1.14 Life in five years for Tajikistan. *Source* Gallup poll (2024)

1.1.7.1 Happiness in Tajikistan

Like Kyrgyzstan, Tajikistan faces economic challenges and political instability that affect its population's well-being. Social cohesion and family networks play crucial roles in maintaining happiness amidst difficulties. The figure shows trends in life satisfaction across five years for Tajikistan over the years (Fig. 1.14).

Tajikistan's life satisfaction scores have shown variability over the years: the scores have ranged from a low of 5.8 in multiple years (2009, 2011, 2012) to a high of 7.9 in 2020. In recent years, relatively stable scores ranging from 7.1–7.2 have been reported, indicating a period of moderate life satisfaction.

The figure shows the Happy Planet Index (HPI) data for Tajikistan from 2006–2021, along with its global ranking in each respective year (Table 1.7).

Tajikistan's HPI rank ranged from 13th (in 2017) to 73rd (in 2011), with a rank of 27th in 2021. The HPI score ranged from a low of 36.48 in 2011 to a peak of 50.55 in 2017. In 2021, the HPI score for Tajikistan was 47.77.

From 2006–2010, Tajikistan's HPI scores fluctuated, generally ranging from the mid-30 s to the mid-40 s, indicating variations in well-being and ecological sustainability efforts during this period. From 2011–2017, significant improvements were observed, with scores increasing from the mid-30 s to over 50 in 2017, reflecting enhancements in well-being and possibly more efficient use of ecological resources. From 2018 to 2021, the scores stabilized around the high 40 s, indicating sustained levels of well-being and ecological balance despite minor fluctuations.

1.1.8 General Information About Turkmenistan

Turkmenistan is a Central Asian country bordering Kazakhstan to the northwest, Uzbekistan to the north and east, Afghanistan to the southeast, Iran to the south, and the Caspian Sea to the west. Turkmenistan's territory is approximately 491,200 sq km. Turkmenistan is predominantly desert and semidesert, with the Karakum Desert covering approximately 80% of the country. The country has significant natural gas

Table 1.7 HPI Rankings for Tajikistan

	HPI	HPI Rank
2006	38,97	
2007	37,68	56
2008	43,40	25
2009	39,40	53
2010	37,27	61
2011	36,48	73
2012	38,50	63
2013	42,57	40
2014	41,85	50
2015	44,04	37
2016	44,10	37
2017	50,55	13
2018	48,19	26
2019	48,36	29
2020	44,72	43
2021	47,77	27

Source Happy Planet Index (2022)

reserves and exports, which form the backbone of its economy. It also has some oil reserves (Fig. 1.15).

The GDP per capita in Turkmenistan is estimated to be approximately $6,000, and Turkmenistan's HDI score is 0.744, which indicates high human development. The country ranked 94th out of 193 countries. The population is approximately 6 million people. Turkmen constitute the largest ethnic group, followed by Uzbeks, Russians, and others.

Few studies have been conducted on challenging circumstances during the transition period, both economically and politically in Turkmenistan. The study is

Fig. 1.15 Map of Turkmenistan

evidenced by the highest levels of dissatisfaction with household income (32.3% very dissatisfied, 8.3% somewhat dissatisfied), housing (14.6% very dissatisfied, 24% somewhat dissatisfied), standard of living (6.3% very dissatisfied, 25.3% somewhat dissatisfied), job (12% very dissatisfied, 13.4% somewhat dissatisfied), and social welfare (10.9% very dissatisfied, 8.8% somewhat dissatisfied). Additionally, a notable proportion of respondents indicated neither satisfaction nor dissatisfaction with the condition of the environment (32.5%), followed by housing (23.5%), social welfare (21.8%), and their job (17.3%) (Timur, 2006). Dadabaev (2007)'s paper on the Asia Barometer project revealed that people's desires and hopes are closely linked to improving their well-being in Turkmenistan.

1.1.9 *Happiness in Turkmenistan*

The figure illustrates Turkmenistan's life satisfaction scores over the years, reflecting perceptions of life evaluations over five years among its population. Life satisfaction scores over five years, such as those indicated for Turkmenistan from 2009–2019, provide insights into how individuals perceive their overall quality of life, encompassing factors such as economic conditions, social stability, healthcare access, etc. Turkmenistan's life satisfaction scores have shown variation over the years, ranging from a high value of 8.6 in 2009 and 2016 to lower values of approximately 7.0 in 2017. In 2019 had a score of 8.0, indicating a relatively high level of life satisfaction, which may reflect improvements in certain aspects of societal conditions during that period (Fig. 1.16).

With a more closed-off political system and economy, Turkmenistan's citizens may have limited access to outside influences but are also shielded from certain

Fig. 1.16 Life evaluations over five years among Turkmenistan people. *Source* Gallup Poll (2024)

Table 1.8 HPI rankings for Turkmenistan

	HPI	HPI rank
2009	32,35	80
2010	30,23	92
2011	27,41	114
2012	25,42	125
2013	24,62	123
2014	26,69	120
2015	26,08	122
2016	27,08	117
2017	24,47	136
2018	21,11	138
2019	24,86	128
2020	25,86	130
2021	25,61	129

Source Happy Planet Index (2022)

global pressures. However, reliable data on happiness in Turkmenistan are scarce because of the government's tight control over information.

The table shows the Happy Planet Index (HPI) scores and ranks for Turkmenistan from 2009–2021 (Table 1.8).

The HPI score ranged from a low of 21.11 in 2018 to a peak of 32.35 in 2009. In 2021, the HPI score for Turkmenistan was 25.61. From 2009 to 2011, Turkmenistan's HPI scores decreased from 32.35 in 2009 to 27.41 in 2011, indicating a decrease in perceived well-being and sustainability efforts during this period. From 2012–2018, scores continued to fluctuate, generally remaining below 30, with a notable drop to 21.11 in 2018, possibly reflecting environmental challenges or economic factors impacting well-being. In recent years, scores have stabilized around the mid-20 s, indicating a period of relative stability in sustainable well-being measures.

The HPI rank provides context by comparing Turkmenistan's score to those of other countries. A lower rank indicates a higher level of sustainable well-being relative to other nations. Turkmenistan's HPI rank ranged from 80th (in 2009) to 138th (in 2018), with a rank of 129th in 2021.

1.2 Conclusion

The analysis of happiness and life satisfaction in Central Asia reveals a complex interplay of historical, economic, and social factors that shape the well-being of individuals across the region. The transition from centrally planned economies to market-oriented systems has resulted in varied outcomes, with countries like Kazakhstan experiencing significant economic growth and achieving high human development status, while others, such as Kyrgyzstan and Tajikistan, continue to face challenges related to political instability and resource scarcity.

The disparities in quality of life highlight the importance of not only economic growth but also the equitable distribution of resources and opportunities among the population. Furthermore, the role of social capital, governance, and public sector employment emerges as critical components influencing subjective well-being. As Central Asian countries navigate their unique paths toward development, understanding these dynamics will be essential for fostering environments that promote happiness and improve the overall quality of life for their citizens. The importance of traditional values, social cohesion, and family in shaping happiness is emphasized, suggesting that cultural context significantly modulates well-being outcomes in Central Asia. This nuanced view complements Western literature but highlights the need for context-specific understanding. Political restrictions and information control challenge data collection, affecting reliability and comparability (Dadabaev, 2007). Innovative qualitative and mixed-method approaches could complement quantitative surveys.

In conclusion, future research on QoL in Central Asia should prioritize cross-country comparative studies to examine how cultural, economic, and political factors shape well-being across the region, identifying both shared patterns and nation-specific variations. Longitudinal studies are needed to establish causal relationships between socioeconomic changes—such as remittances, governance reforms, and shifts in social capital—and fluctuations in happiness levels over time. Additionally, ethnographic and qualitative research could provide deeper insights into indigenous conceptions of well-being, moving beyond Western-centric metrics. These research directions would enhance understanding of happiness in post-Soviet societies while contributing to broader global discussions on subjective well-being.

References

Analytical Tables—Agency on Statistics Under the President of the Republic of Tajikistan. (2023). *Агентии омори назди Президенти Ҷумҳурии Тоҷикистон* (blog). https://www.stat.tj/en/analytical-tables/

Batsaikhan, U., & Dabrowski, M. (2017). Central Asia—Twenty-Five Years after the Breakup of the USSR. *Russian Journal of Economics, 3*(3), 296–320.

Collins, K., & Gambrel, R. (2017). Corruption and Popular Support for Democracy and Government in Transitional Contexts: The Case of Kyrgyzstan. *Europe-Asia Studies, 69*(8), 1280–1309. https://doi.org/10.1080/09668136.2017.1384449

Dadabaev, T. (2007). Trajectories of Political Development and Public Choices in Turkmenistan. *Asian Affairs: An American Review, 34*(3), 131–150. https://doi.org/10.3200/AAFS.34.3.131-150

Demircioglu, M. A., & Sharipova, D. (2023). Does Public Sector Employment Matter for Subjective Well-Being? The Case of Kazakhstan. *International Journal of Public Administration*, 1–16.

Diener, A. C. (2005). Kazakhstan's Kin State Diaspora: Settlement Planning and the Oralman Dilemma. *Europe-Asia Studies, 57*(2), 327–348. https://doi.org/10.1080/09668130500052005
Gallup Organization. (2024). *The Gallup Organization.*
Haerpfer, C., Inglehart, R., Moreno, A., Welzel, C., Kizilova, K., Diez-Medrano J., M. Lagos, P. Norris, E. Ponarin & B. Puranen (Eds.). (2022). World Values Survey: Madrid, Spain & Vienna, Austria: JD Systems Institute & WVSA Secretariat. https://doi.org/10.14281/18241.24
Helliwell, J., Layard, R., & Sachs, J. (2022). *World Happiness Report 2022.* Sustainable Development Solutions Network.
Inoguchi, T., & Fujii, S. (2012). *The Quality of Life in Asia: A Comparison of Quality of Life in Asia.* Springer Science & Business Media.
Jamanbalayeva, S., & Tlenchiyeva, S. (2024). Happiness in Kazakhstan. *International Journal of Happiness and Development, 8*(4), 376–393.
Kim, S. (2023). Comparison of Happiness Levels in Central Asian Countries. *Journal of the Korea Society of Computer and Information, 28*(6), 145–152.
Kudebayeva, A., Sharipova, A., & Sharipova, D. (2022). Social Capital and Subjective Well-Being in Central Asia. *Europe-Asia Studies, 74*(1), 101–124. https://doi.org/10.1080/09668136.2021.1973965
Laruelle, M., Huchet, J. -F., Peyrouse, S., & Balci, B. (2010). Why Central Asia? The Strategic Rationale of Indian and Chinese Involvement in the Region. In Laruelle, M., Huchet, J. -F., Peyrouse, S., & Balci, B. (Eds.), *China and India in Central Asia*, edited by Marlène Laruelle, Jean-François Huchet, Sébastien Peyrouse, and Bayram Balci (pp. 1–6). Palgrave Macmillan US. https://doi.org/10.1057/9780230114357_1
Li, J., Chen, Y., Li, Z., & Huang, X. (2019). Low-Carbon Economic Development in Central Asia Based on LMDI Decomposition and Comparative Decoupling Analyses. *Journal of Arid Land, 11*(4), 513–524. https://doi.org/10.1007/s40333-019-0063-0
Makulbayeva, G. A., Davletbayeva, Zh. Zh., & Dyussenov, M. M. (2023). *Subjective Well-Being in Central Asia: Rural-Urban Differences, 145*(4), 363–373.
Marks, N., Abdallah, S., Simms, A., & Thompson, S. (2022). *The (un)happy Planet Index: An Index of Human Well-Being and Ecological Impact*. NEF.
Megoran, N. (2010). The Uzbekistan-Kyrgyzstan Boundary: Stalin's Cartography, Post-Soviet Geography. *Borderliness and Borderlands: Political Oddities at the Edge of the Nation-State*, 33–52.
Migration and Development Brief 38 | KNOMAD. (2023). *2023.* https://knomad.org/publication/migration-and-development-brief-38
Naghdi, Y., Amirtaemeh, H., & Kaghazian, S. (2021). The Puzzle of the Relationship between Economic Growth and Happiness. *Economic Analysis, 54*(1), 1–12.
Nurdinova, S. (2024). Happiness in Uzbekistan. *International Journal of Happiness and Development, 8*(4), 436–449.
Omarova, A., & Kenzhakimov, G. (2023). Sociological Measurement of the Happiness Index in Central Asian Countries. *Journal of Community Positive Practices, 1*, 17–28.
Population—Official Statistics—Statistics of the Kyrgyz Republic. (2024). *2024.* https://stat.gov.kg/en/statistics/naselenie/
Population of the Republic of Kazakhstan by Gender and Type of Locality. (2024, April 1). *2024.* https://stat.gov.kz/en/industries/social-statistics/demography/publications/159623/
Sharipova, D., & Kudebayeva, A. (2023a). Changing Well-Being in Central Asia: Evidence from Kazakhstan and Kyrgyzstan. *Journal of Happiness Studies, 24*(3), 1233–1260.
Sharipova, D., & Kudebayeva, A. (2023b). Changing Well-Being in Central Asia: Evidence from Kazakhstan and Kyrgyzstan. *Journal of Happiness Studies,* 24(3), 1233–1260. https://doi.org/10.1007/s10902-022-00607-1
Spechler, M. C. (2008). The Economies of Central Asia: A Survey. *Comparative Economic Studies, 50*(1), 30–52. https://doi.org/10.1057/ces.2008.3
Statistical Agency of Uzbekistan, Demografiya. (2024). *2024.* https://stat.uz/uz/rasmiy-statistika/demography-2

Timur, D. (2006). Living Conditions, Intra-Societal Trust, and Public Concerns in Post-Socialist Turkmenistan. *Central Asia and the Caucasus, 4*(40), 122–132.

Uzbekistan Pilot Multidimensional Poverty Index Report 2023: Poverty and Deprivation Analysis Using the Multidimensional Poverty Index (MPI) | OPHI. (2023). *2023*. https://ophi.org.uk/publications/Uzbekistan-MPI-2023

Veenhoven, R. *Rank report Happy Life Years in Nations 2010–2019*, World Database of Happiness, Erasmus University Rotterdam, The Netherlands. https://worlddatabaseofhappiness.eur.nl/

World Bank Open Data. (2024). https://data.worldbank.org

Chapter 2
Quality of Life Issues in Central Asia

Abstract Quality of life in Central Asia is shaped by a complex interplay of economic, political, environmental, and sociocultural factors. Since the collapse of the Soviet Union, challenges such as poverty, governance deficits, environmental degradation, and social inequality continue to affect well-being. Economically, disparities exist between resource-rich Kazakhstan and remittance-dependent Kyrgyzstan and Tajikistan, limited job opportunities drive labor migration. Environmental crises, the Aral Sea disaster and climate-induced water scarcity, further threaten health and livelihoods. Culturally, traditional norms, ethnic diversity, and gender roles influence life satisfaction. Patriarchal structures limit women's opportunities, while urbanization widens gaps between modernized cities and marginalized rural areas. Despite these challenges, incremental reforms in Uzbekistan and Kazakhstan's green energy initiatives offer cautious optimism. This analysis underscores the need for inclusive policies addressing economic diversification, environmental sustainability, and social equity to enhance regional quality of life.

Keywords Central Asia · Quality of life · Inequality · Governance · Environment · Sociocultural norms

2.1 Introduction

This chapter investigates Quality of life (QoL) issues in Central Asia, economic, political, environmental, and social factors affecting life satisfaction. Elders in Central Asia promote "harmony, unity, and moral socialization" as core community values, fostering mutual obligations among members. With the state failing to meet their needs, they established cooperatives to provide social security and solidarity. Operating autonomously, these elders blend proactive advocacy with traditional community care duties. This chapter highlights community's central role in shaping well-being across Central Asia. From religious networks to Kyrgyz villagers' conceptions

S. Nurdinova, *Happiness and Life Satisfaction in Central Asia*, Quality of Life in Asia 24, https://doi.org/10.1007/978-981-95-3082-3_2

of authority and Tajiks' and Uzbeks' coping strategies, diverse community understandings emerge as vital. These local perspectives challenge assumptions about what makes life meaningful (Montgomery, 2013).

The region exhibits striking contrasts—from Kazakhstan's economic dominance to the lagging economies of Kyrgyzstan and Tajikistan, and from Uzbekistan's reform-driven growth to Turkmenistan's closed authoritarianism. These variations are further shaped by informal patronage networks, which permeate state institutions, and by differing societal priorities, with some nations emphasizing economic stability while others prioritize social progress or environmental protection. Central Asia faces mounting pressures from climate change, with rising temperatures triggering disasters that threaten livelihoods and food security. Healthcare systems, though undergoing reforms, remain uneven in quality and accessibility, reflecting broader inequalities in human development. Against this backdrop, the region's future hinges on its ability to reconcile economic ambitions with governance transparency, social cohesion, and environmental sustainability.

Conceptually, Central Asia exposes gaps in mainstream QoL theories, particularly their underappreciation of how informal economies and kinship structures recalibrate the impact of unemployment, or how religiosity operates as both a psychological resource and a societal organizer. The region's healthcare efficiency paradox—achieving better outcomes with lower spending—further challenges assumptions about the linear relationship between resource inputs and well-being outputs.

2.1.1 Economic Challenges and Opportunities

The economic landscape of Central Asia differs in development levels. Kazakhstan maintains regional economic dominance with a GDP per capita of approximately $14,149. Uzbekistan follows at roughly $3113, demonstrating gradual growth through economic reforms and strategic positioning in regional trade networks. Kyrgyzstan and Tajikistan trail significantly with estimates of $2471 and $1432 respectively ('IMF Data', 2025). In Central Asia, clan influence depends on powerful individuals and familial loyalty, with economic crises reinforcing informal patronage networks. These networks permeate state institutions, as seen in Kyrgyzstan's nepotistic bureaucracy under Bakiyev, Kazakhstan's tribal clientelism under Nazarbayev, and Turkmenistan's state-criminal collusion. Uzbekistan, by contrast, co-opts traditional mahallas—once autonomous social units—to extend state control, embedding officials directly into local communities (Kamrava, 2020).

The comparative analysis of societal value priorities across Central Asian states reveals significant cross-national variation in public preferences regarding economic stability versus social progress. As the data demonstrate, Uzbekistan exhibits a pronounced emphasis on developing a more humane society (35.3%), substantially exceeding regional averages and contrasting sharply with Kyrgyzstan's predominant concern for economic stability (26%). Kazakhstan presents the most balanced

Table 2.1 Societal values in Central Asia

	Kazakhstan	Kyrgyzstan	Tajikistan	Uzbekistan
A stable economy	18	26	23	16,9
Progress toward a less impersonal and more humane society	27,7	19,9	22,9	35,3
Progress toward a society in which Ideas count more than money	22,6	18	21,9	22,1

Source World Values Survey (2022)

distribution of priorities, with near-equal valuation of humane society (27.7%) and idea-centric progress (22.6%) (Table 2.1).

Public discontent and protests are not unique to Kazakhstan. In Kyrgyzstan, demonstrations are a common means of voicing grievances. Elsewhere, governments react differently: in Turkmenistan, rare protests over economic hardships reveal the severity of its crisis, while Uzbekistan has begun addressing local criticisms. Tajikistan, however, has taken an authoritarian approach—suppressing dissent, exiling opposition groups, and fueling distrust without diminishing the appeal of political Islam (Stronski & Zanca, 2019).

2.1.2 Cultural and Social Dimensions

While material exchanges is measured, understanding the moral and affective dimensions of a "good life" demands nuanced interpretation. Well-being emerges through social navigation, as individuals and communities adapt their visions in response to changing environments. These negotiations are never isolated but always relational, requiring deep contextual understanding to fully grasp how people construct meaning in their lives (Montgomery, 2013). Gallup Poll data shows Uzbekistan has the highest freedom choice satisfaction (91%) followed by Turkmenistan and Tajikistan (69% and 67%). Kyrgyzstan and Kazakhstan fall in between 77 and 74%. Although the general health of the population remains suboptimal, Kyrgyzstan did not experience the sharp rise in mid-life male mortality observed in other CIS countries. Health status undoubtedly influences overall well-being, but cultural factors—particularly the predominance of Sunni Islam—may also play a significant role. Further research is necessary to explore the reasons behind Kyrgyzstan's higher levels of subjective life satisfaction compared to neighboring post-Soviet states (Abbott et al., 2011).

Kazakhstan, with the smallest titular nation share (68% Kazakhs vs. 73% Kyrgyz and 84% Uzbeks), underwent the most repressive nation-building, resulting in weaker local affiliations. In contrast, Kyrgyzstan's more democratic approach and Uzbekistan's international isolation fostered stronger local and national identities. Uzbekistan shows the highest patriotism (94% willing to fight for their country, 88% feeling "very proud"), while Kazakhstan exhibits greater alienation, with weaker ties to both

Central Asia and the global community (Haerpfer & Kizilova 2020). Religion holds deep significance in Uzbekistan, with 39.8% of respondents rating God's importance as "10" on a scale from 1 (not important) to 10 (very important). An overwhelming majority (87.9%) rated it between 6 and 10, while fewer than 10% gave ratings of 1 to 5 (Dadabaev, 2007a, 2007b).

2.1.3 Environmental and Climate Issues

Central Asia has faced climate-related disasters in recent years. The region, is warming at a rate exceeding the global average, has witnessed a rise in sudden-onset disasters—such as flash floods, mudflows, and extreme rainfall events—linked to anthropogenic climate change. For instance, in 2020 alone, catastrophic flooding in Uzbekistan and Kazakhstan triggered 70,000 and 32,000 new displacements, respectively.

Populations residing in grassland ecosystems are particularly vulnerable, facing higher exposure to torrential rains and floods compared to those in arid zones. These disasters pose severe threats to livelihood security, as recurrent storms, droughts, wildfires, and mudflows degrade agricultural productivity, thereby amplifying food insecurity. The compounding effects of environmental degradation and economic instability create a feedback loop that undermines long-term resilience, particularly for rural and marginalized communities (McAuliffe & Triandafyllidou, 2022).

Kazakhstan ranks 61st (33.43 points) in the 2025 Climate Change Performance Index (CCPI), reflecting its status as a very low performer in climate mitigation efforts. The country scores particularly poorly in GHG emissions, renewable energy adoption, and energy efficiency, while receiving only marginally better ratings in climate policy. Although Kazakhstan has formulated a Carbon Neutrality Strategy (2060) and experts acknowledge progress in its operationalization, significant shortcomings persist. A key criticism is the absence of sector-specific decarbonization targets, which undermines the strategy's feasibility (Burck et al., 2024).

Furthermore, while the plan emphasizes reducing coal dependency and scaling up renewable energy, it simultaneously promotes natural gas as a transitional fuel and includes nuclear power in its long-term energy mix—an approach that climate analysts view as inconsistent with rapid decarbonization. Most concerning is Kazakhstan's intention to expand coal capacity by 6 GW by 2030, despite its 2060 coal phase-out pledge, a contradiction that highlights the tension between short-term fossil fuel interests and long-term climate commitments. As one of the top 10 global holders of developed coal reserves and with plans to increase oil and gas production, Kazakhstan's climate policy remains heavily influenced by its fossil fuel-dependent economy, raising doubts about its ability to align with the Paris Agreement's 1.5 °C pathway.

Uzbekistan has fallen six places in the 2025 Climate Change Performance Index (CCPI), ranking 54th with a score of 44.51 (Burck et al., 2023). The country earns very low ratings in GHG emissions and renewable energy adoption, while receiving only medium scores in energy use and climate policy—highlighting a critical lag in transitioning away from fossil fuels.

Uzbekistan's energy sector remains heavily dependent on natural gas, which accounts for 83% of total energy supply, alongside a significant reliance on coal power—a major contributor to the country's high per capita emissions. Despite recent policy declarations supporting renewable energy expansion, progress remains slow and inconsistent, with renewables constituting a negligible share of the energy mix. This continued fossil fuel dependence not only undermines Uzbekistan's climate commitments but also exacerbates air pollution and energy insecurity, particularly in urban centers (Burck et al., 2024).

The figure reveals differences in public attitudes toward environmental protection across four Central Asian countries—Kazakhstan, Kyrgyzstan, Tajikistan, and Uzbekistan. Kyrgyzstan stands out with 61.7% of respondents prioritizing environmental protection, even at the expense of economic growth and jobs. Kyrgyzstan and Tajikistan (both 43.7%) demonstrate the lowest support environmental issues. Uzbekistan (46.8%) show near-majority support for environmental prioritization, likely influenced by Tashkent's air quality and the Aral Sea disaster.

2.1.4 Healthcare and Access to Medical Services

The decentralization of hospital management in post-Soviet Central Asia has necessitated significant development of managerial capacities within healthcare institutions. As integral components of a complex health system, hospitals must adapt to evolving patient needs at different stages of organizational development. The digital transformation of healthcare has empowered patients and shifted care paradigms from physician-centered approaches to organizational care processes. Effective hospital management now requires the ability to identify patient values and implement adaptive management models. Strategic management plays a pivotal role in translating organizational objectives into actionable decisions, enabling healthcare professionals to deliver meaningful outcomes through coordinated efforts (Kosherbayeva et al., 2020).

Access to quality healthcare remains a critical quality of life issue across Central Asia. Kazakhstan has the most advanced medical facilities (Eriksen et al., 2022).

Kyrgyzstan struggle with severe shortages of doctors and medicines, particularly in remote regions. Kyrgyzstan's maternal mortality ratio (MMR) of 50.4 per 100,000 live births (2020) and infant mortality rate (IMR) of 15.6 per 1000 live births (2021) highlight gaps in reproductive healthcare (World Health Organization, 2021).

Uzbekistan has initiated reforms to improve primary care, yet out-of-pocket expenses remain high. Uzbekistan's maternal mortality ratio (MMR) of 30.2 per 100,000 live births (2020) compared to the Central Asian average of 24.3. Turkmenistan's closed system lacks transparency, with reports of medicine shortages and restricted treatment options.

Education serves as a potential mechanism for enhancing quality of life in Central Asia. The region variable exhibits a statistically significant negative effect on efficiency scores, indicating that Central Asian countries demonstrate higher efficiency performance compared to Europe. This finding implies a discernible regional influence, possibly attributable to superior healthcare systems, more advanced medical technology, and a lower proportion of GDP allocated to health expenditures in Central Asia (Hsu, 2013).

2.2 Conclusion

The economic, social, and environmental landscapes of Central Asia reveal a region marked by contrasts and evolving challenges. Economically, Kazakhstan maintains dominance with its higher GDP per capita, while Uzbekistan demonstrates gradual growth through reforms, and Kyrgyzstan and Tajikistan lag behind. These disparities are further complicated by entrenched patronage networks and clan-based governance, which shape political and economic structures differently across the region—from Kyrgyzstan's nepotistic bureaucracy to Uzbekistan's co-optation of traditional *mahallas*.

Societal values also diverge significantly, with Uzbekistan prioritizing a humane society, Kyrgyzstan emphasizing economic stability, and Kazakhstan balancing multiple priorities. Public discontent manifests in varied ways, from protests in Kyrgyzstan to authoritarian suppression in Tajikistan, reflecting differing governance approaches. Culturally, religion and national identity play pivotal roles, with Uzbekistan exhibiting strong religiosity and patriotism, while Kazakhstan shows weaker local affiliations due to its repressive nation-building past.

Environmental challenges further strain the region, with climate change exacerbating disasters like floods and droughts, particularly in vulnerable rural areas. Kazakhstan and Uzbekistan's heavy reliance on fossil fuels undermines their climate commitments, despite nominal policy efforts. Public attitudes toward environmental protection vary, with Kyrgyzstan showing the highest support for ecological priorities.

Healthcare systems remain uneven, with Kazakhstan leading in infrastructure while other nations struggle with accessibility and quality. Decentralization and digital transformation are reshaping medical management, yet disparities persist in maternal and infant mortality rates. Education and healthcare efficiency suggest potential pathways for improving well-being, though structural and economic constraints hinder progress. Central Asia's trajectory hinges on balancing economic development, governance reform, social cohesion, and environmental sustainability.

From the perspective of quality of life (QoL) studies, Central Asia presents a compelling case of how post-Soviet transitions, cultural traditions, and environmental pressures interact to shape well-being in ways that both align with and challenge global paradigms. The region's economic disparities—from Kazakhstan's

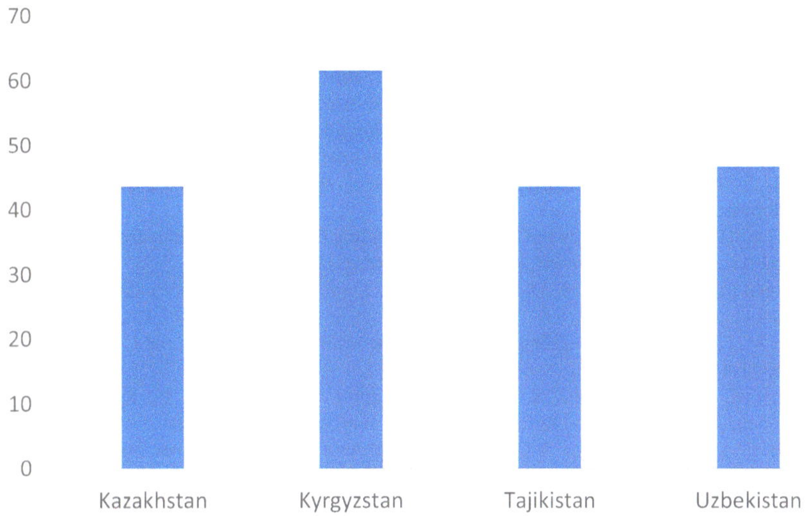

Fig. 2.1 Figure protecting the environment in Central Asia. *Source* World Values Survey (2024)

hydrocarbon-fueled prosperity to Tajikistan's remittance-dependent economy—demonstrate how macro-level factors differentially influence life satisfaction, yet with notable deviations from Western models. While income remains predictive of life satisfaction, the relative resilience of happiness in low-GDP contexts like Kyrgyzstan suggests the buffering role of informal social networks and collectivist values, underscoring the need to expand QoL frameworks beyond material indicators. The persistence of traditional institutions (mahallas, aksakal councils) as alternative welfare systems highlights how culturally embedded social capital mediates state failures—a phenomenon less visible in institutionalized Western contexts. Environmental stressors, particularly climate-induced disasters and the Aral Sea crisis, introduce acute ecological dimensions to QoL that surpass typical Western environmental concerns, demanding integrated models that link sustainability directly to well-being (Fig. 1.1).

References

Abbott, P., Wallace, C., & Sapsford, R. (2011). Surviving the transformation: Social quality in Central Asia and the Caucuses. *Journal of Happiness Studies, 12*(2), 199–223.

Burck, J., Marten, F., Bals, C., & Höhne, N. (2024). *Climate Change Performance Index.*

Burck, J., Marten, F., Bals, C., & Höhne, N. (2025). *Climate Change Performance Index.*

Dadabaev, T. (2007a). How Does Transition Work in Central Asia? Coping with Ideological, Economic and Value System Changes in Uzbekistan. *Central Asian Survey, 26*(3), 407–428.

Dadabaev, T. (2007b). Trajectories of Political Development and Public Choices in Turkmenistan. *Asian Affairs: An American Review, 34*(3), 131–150.

Eriksen, A., Litvinova, Y., & Rechel, B. (2022). Health Systems in Action: Kazakhstan.

Haerpfer, C., Inglehart, R., Moreno, A., Welzel, C., Kizilova, K., Diez-Medrano J., M. Lagos, P. Norris, E. Ponarin & B. Puranen (Eds.). (2022). World Values Survey: Madrid, Spain & Vienna, Austria: JD Systems Institute & WVSA Secretariat. https://doi.org/10.14281/18241.24

Haerpfer, C. W., & Kizilova, K. (2020). Values and Transformation in Central Asia. In *Transformation and development: Studies in the Organization for Security and Cooperation in Europe (OSCE) member states* (pp. 7–28). Springer International Publishing.

Helliwell, J., Layard, R., & Sachs, J. (2022). *World Happiness Report 2022.* Sustainable Development Solutions Network.

Hsu, Y.-C. (2013). The Efficiency of Government Spending on Health: Evidence from Europe and Central Asia. *The Social Science Journal, 50*(4), 665–673.

International Monetary Fund. (2025). *World Economic Outlook Database*. International Monetary Fund.

Kamrava, M. (2020). Nation-Building in Central Asia: Institutions, Politics, and Culture. *Muslim World,* 110(1).

Kosherbayeva, L., Kalmakhanov, S., Hailey, D., Pazilov, S., Seiduanova, L., Kozhamkul, R., Jaworzynska, M., Bazhanova, A. E., Juraeva, N., & Jarylkasynova, G. (2020). Rethinking Priorities in Hospital Management: A Case from Central Asia. *Health Policy and Technology, 9*(3), 391–396.

Marks, N., Abdallah, S., Simms, A., & Thompson, S. (2022). *The (un)happy Planet Index: An Index of Human Well-being and Ecological Impact*. NEF.

McAuliffe, M., & Triandafyllidou, A. (2021). *Word Migration Report 2022.*

Montgomery, C. (2013). *Happy City: Transforming Our Lives Through Urban Design.* Penguin.

Population—Official Statistics—Statistics of the Kyrgyz Republic. (2024). *2024.* https://stat.gov.kg/en/statistics/naselenie/

Population of the Republic of Kazakhstan by Gender and Type of Locality (2024, April 1). *2024.* https://stat.gov.kz/en/industries/social-statistics/demography/publications/159623/

Strategy of the Republic of Kazakhstan on Achieving Carbon Neutrality by 2060, app. (2023).

Stronski, P., & Zanca, R. (2019). Societal Change Afoot in Central Asia. *World, 17*(20), 18.

World Health Organization. (2021). *Statistics.* WHO.

Chapter 3
Happiness and Economics in Central Asia

Abstract The study investigates the relationship between economic development and happiness in Central Asia, examining the various factors influencing well-being in the region. It explores the impact of economic growth, income inequality, social policies, and cultural aspects on happiness, providing a comprehensive overview of how economic and social policies can be tailored to enhance overall well-being. The influx of wealth from natural resources has led to significant economic development in countries like Kazakhstan and Turkmenistan, contributing to improved living standards and potential increases in happiness. However, uneven distribution of benefits from economic growth can lead to heightened levels of dissatisfaction in regions with significant income and opportunity disparities. The study utilizes data from the World Values Survey to measure a wide range of socioeconomic variables and employs methods such as the self-reported subjective well-being approach, linear regression analysis to interpret data on happiness and life satisfaction.

Keywords Economic development · Happiness · Central Asia · Income inequality · Subjective well-being · Regression

3.1 Introduction

This chapter explores the dynamics between economic development and happiness in Central Asia, examining both the opportunities and challenges that influence well-being in the region. It investigates the impacts of economic growth, income inequality, social policies, and cultural factors on happiness, providing a comprehensive overview of how economic and social policies can be tailored to enhance well-being. Economic growth is often associated with improvements in living standards, which can contribute to increased happiness. In Central Asia, the influx of wealth from natural resources has led to significant economic development, particularly in Kazakhstan and Turkmenistan. Higher income levels can lead to better access to healthcare, education, and other essential services, all of which are important for well-being. However, economic growth does not always translate directly into increased

S. Nurdinova, *Happiness and Life Satisfaction in Central Asia*, Quality of Life in Asia 24, https://doi.org/10.1007/978-981-95-3082-3_3

happiness. In many cases, the benefits of growth are unevenly distributed. Regions with significant disparities in income and opportunities can experience heightened levels of dissatisfaction, despite overall economic progress.

The World Values Survey provided data were used. A wide range of socioeconomic variables, such as income scale, income inequality, important of work, freedom of choice, etc., are measured using the survey's basic module. Happiness and life satisfaction are the dependent variables in the study, the self-reported subjective well-being approach, and ordered probit/logit, or linear regression analysis are the most popular methods for interpreting the data on happiness and life satisfaction (Selim, 2008; Veenhoven, 2016).

3.1.1 Economic Development and Happiness in Kazakhstan

Since the 2000s, Kazakhstan has experienced significant economic growth driven by market-oriented reforms, abundant mineral resource extraction, and strong foreign direct investment (FDI) (Kalyuzhnova & Patterson, 2016). This growth has transformed the country into an upper middle-income economy, increasing living standards and reducing poverty. The 2024 economic forecast anticipates a growth slowdown to 3.4%, with a rebound to 4.7% in 2025 due to increased oil production. Additionally, Kazakhstan's GDP is expected to grow by 3.8% in 2024 and 5.3% in 2025, with per capita GDP growth expected at 2.0% in 2024 and 3.4% in 2025.

Despite this growth, Kazakhstan continues to face economic challenges rooted in the Soviet era, including weak trade links with other Central Asian states and a cumbersome regulatory system that impedes business growth. The country has set a goal to become one of the 30 most developed countries in the world by 2050, but to achieve this goal it will need to overcome significant challenges.

The analysis of the data from Waves 6 and 7 provides a comprehensive understanding of the factors influencing life satisfaction and happiness among respondents in Kazakhstan. The results highlight various socioeconomic and individual factors that contribute to well-being, with significant insights into the impact of marital status, employment, income, freedom of choice, and other variables. To support these findings, it is essential to relate them to the literature on well-being, happiness, and life satisfaction (Table 3.1).

The data from Wave 6 provide insights into various aspects of the respondents' lives. The mean happiness score was 3.20 (std. dev. 0.63) on a scale of 1–4, indicating a moderate level of happiness. Life satisfaction had a higher mean of 7.25 (std. dev. 2.10) on a scale of 1–10, suggesting a relatively high level of overall life satisfaction. The mean gender value of 0.39 indicates that approximately 39.6% of the respondents are male.

In terms of marital status, the majority (82.6%) were married, 17.4% were divorced, and 19.8% were single. With respect to employment, 63.93% were employed, 6.4% were unemployed, and 29.67% were out of the labor force. The average income scale score is 5.30, suggesting that respondents generally fall around

Table 3.1 Variable definitions

Variable	Definition
Life satisfaction	Measures overall satisfaction with life. Respondents rate their satisfaction on a scale from 1 (completely dissatisfied) to 10 (completely satisfied)
Happiness	Assesses overall happiness. Respondents indicate their happiness level on a scale from 1 (not at all happy) to 4 (very happy)
Gender	Indicates the respondent's gender, where 0 typically represents female and 1 represents male
Marital status	Represents marital status as a set of dummy variables. Each status (married, single, divorced) is coded as 1 or 0
Employment status	Employment status is represented by a set of dummy variables. Categories include: Out of Labor Market (retired/pensioned, homemaker, student), Unemployed (actively seeking employment), and Employed (full-time, part-time, or self-employed)
Income scale	Indicates the household's income level on a scale from 1 (lowest income group) to 10 (highest income group) in the respondent's country
Importance of work	Measures how important work is to the respondent, rated on a scale from 1 (very important) to 10 (not at all important)
Freedom of choice	Assesses the level of freedom and control the respondent feels they have, rated from 1 (no choice at all) to 10 (the highest freedom)
Education level	Represents the highest educational attainment of the respondent, ranging from early childhood education (0) to the highest educational level achieved
Age	The respondent's age in years
Age squared	The square of the respondent's age, obtained by multiplying their age by itself
Income equality	Views on income equality, rated from 1 (incomes should be made more equal) to 10 (incomes should not be made more equal)
Government responsibility	Opinion on the level of government responsibility, rated from 1 (the government should take more responsibility) to 10 (the government should not take responsibility)
Satisfaction with politics	Measures satisfaction with the political system, rated from 1 (completely dissatisfied) to 10 (completely satisfied)

the middle of the income scale. The average importance placed on work is 1.59, suggesting that work is generally considered of moderate importance by the respondents. The average score for freedom of choice is 7.04, indicating that respondents generally feel that they have a relatively high level of freedom. The mean educational level of 6.69 suggests that respondents generally have a moderate level of education. The average age is 40.02 years, with a wide range spanning from 18–88 years. The mean of age squared is 1836.76, which, combined with the standard deviation, reflects the quadratic relationship of age and its impact on various outcomes. The average perception of income equality is 5.34, suggesting a mid-range view of how equitable income distribution is perceived.

In Wave 7, the mean happiness score was 3.22 (std. dev. 0.61) on a scale of 1–4, which was slightly higher than that in Wave 6. Life satisfaction had a mean of 7.06 (std. dev. 2.09) on a scale of 1–10, which was slightly lower than that in Wave 6. The proportion of respondents who were married decreased to 66.53%, while the proportion of divorced respondents increased to 19.05%, and that of single respondents decreased to 14.42%. The standard deviations for these proportions indicate variability in marital status, similar to Wave 6. Employment status remained relatively stable, with 68.21% employed, 4.95% unemployed, and 26.84% out of the labor force. The mean income scale rating increased to 5.60(std. dev. 1.66) on a scale of 1–10, indicating a slight improvement in income satisfaction. The importance of work increased slightly, with a mean rating of 1.65 (std. dev. 0.78) on a scale of 1–4. The mean rating for freedom of choice decreased to 6.91 (standard deviation 2.20) on a scale of 1–10 but still indicated a relatively high level of perceived freedom (Table 3.2).

The average educational level decreased to 4.81 (std. dev. 1.72) on a scale of 1–9, potentially due to changes in the sample composition. The mean age of the respondents increased to 41.67 years (std. dev. 13.90), with ages ranging from 18–88 years. New variables in Wave 7 included the government's responsibility, with a mean rating of 4.82 (std. dev. 2.83) on a scale of 1–10, and satisfaction with politics, with a mean rating of 6.45 (std. dev. 2.26) on a scale of 1–10. Overall, the statistics from both waves provide valuable insights into the respondents' well-being, employment, marital status, and perceptions of various aspects of their lives. The standard deviations indicate variability within the sample, highlighting the diversity of experiences and opinions.

The regression results in Table 3.3 provide insights into the factors influencing life satisfaction and happiness among the sample of 1500 individuals. Each coefficient represents the impact of a specific variable on life satisfaction and happiness, adjusted for other variables in the model.

Marital status indicates that being divorced significantly reduces life satisfaction ($\beta = -0.61$) compared with being married.

Employment status reveals that being unemployed significantly decreases life satisfaction ($\beta = -0.60$). Being employed also reduces life satisfaction ($\beta = -0.34$).

The income scale positively influences life satisfaction ($\beta = 0.18$), indicating that higher income generally enhances life satisfaction more significantly than happiness does.

The coefficient for the importance of work is $\beta = 0.16$, indicating a statistically significant positive association with life satisfaction. When people consider work to be less important, they are more satisfied with their life. Freedom of choice, which is statistically significant, is positively associated with life satisfaction. Income equality ($\beta = 0.05$) also contributes positively to life satisfaction, indicating that people believe that income should not be more equal when they are more satisfied with their lives.

The R-squared value is 0.19, indicating that the model explains approximately 19.32% of the variance in life satisfaction based on the included variables.

Being single has a smaller negative impact on happiness ($\beta = -0.11$). Compared with being in the reference group, being divorced reduces the happiness level. Compared with being out of the labor force, being unemployed or employed has

Table 3.2 Descriptive statistics

Variable	Wave 6 Mean	Wave 6 Std. Dev	Wave 7 Mean	Wave 7 Std. Dev	Min	Max
Happiness	3.20	0.63	3.22	0.61	1	4
Life satisfaction	7.25	2.10	7.06	2.09	1	10
Gender	0.40	0.49	0.45	0.50	0	1
Marital status						
– Divorced	0.17	0.38	0.19	0.39	0	1
– Married	0.83	0.38	0.67	0.47	0	1
– Single	0.20	0.40	0.14	0.35	0	1
Employment status						
– Unemployed	0.06	0.24	0.05	0.22	0	1
– Employed	0.64	0.48	0.68	0.47	0	1
– Out of labor market	0.30	0.46	0.27	0.44	0	1
Income scale	5.30	1.95	5.60	1.66	1	10
Importance of Work	1.59	0.85	1.65	0.78	1	4
Freedom of choice	7.04	2.34	6.91	2.20	1	10
Educational level	6.69	1.85	4.81	1.72	1	9
Age	40.02	15.35	41.67	13.90	18	88
Age squared	1836.76	1406.21	1929.37	1271.73	32 4	7744
Income equality	5.34	2.92			1	10
Government's responsibility	4.82	2.83	1.00	10.00		
Satisfaction with politics			6.45	2.26	1	10
N	1500		950			

a moderate negative effect on happiness. Freedom of choice is positively associated with happiness. Income equality also contributes weakly and statistically significantly positively to happiness.

The table shows that the regression results offer a detailed view of the factors influencing life satisfaction and happiness within a sample of 950 individuals. Each coefficient represents the impact of a specific variable on life satisfaction and happiness, accounting for other variables in the model. The income scale has a significant positive influence on life satisfaction ($\beta = 0.16$), indicating that higher income generally enhances life satisfaction.

Table 3.3 Factors affecting subjective well-being in Kazakhstan

Variable	Life satisfaction	Happiness
Gender	0.03	0.01
Marital status		
Divorced	−0.61***	−0.25***
Married	(omitted)	(omitted)
Single	−0.24	−0.11*
Employment status		
Unemployed	−0.60**	−0.16*
Employed	−0.34*	−0.19***
Out of labor market	(omitted)	(omitted)
Income scale	0.18***	0.02
Importance of work	0.16*	−0.01
Freedom of choice	0.27***	0.04***
Educational level	0.02	0.01
Age	−0.01	−0.01
Age squared	0.00	0.00
Income equality	0.05*	0.01*
Constant (_cons)	4.53***	3.21***
N	1500	1500
R^2	0.19	0.09

Legend * $P < 0.05$; ** $P < 0.01$; *** $P < 0.001$

Freedom of choice has a positive effect on life satisfaction ($\beta = 0.51$). Additionally, satisfaction with politics positively influences life satisfaction ($\beta = 0.17$). Sociodemographic variables such as age, gender, marital status and employment status have statistically insignificant effects on life satisfaction. An R-squared value of 0.42 indicates that the regression model explains approximately 41.64% of the variance in the dependent variable.

The importance of work is negatively associated with happiness ($\beta = -0.05$), suggesting that placing greater importance on work may slightly increase levels of happiness. Freedom of choice has a positive effect on happiness ($\beta = 0.04$), highlighting the significant role that perceived freedom plays in enhancing well-being. Educational level is positively associated with happiness ($\beta = 0.03$) indicating that higher education levels tend to contribute to higher levels of happiness. This finding supports the literature that higher education levels contribute positively to well-being and happiness, although the effect on life satisfaction can vary depending on individual circumstances (Oreopoulos, 2008). Satisfaction with political performance suggests that higher satisfaction with political circumstances tends to correlate with higher levels of overall well-being. The findings support the previous literature that political stability and satisfaction with governance can enhance overall life

Table 3.4 Factors affecting subjective well-being

Variable	Life satisfaction	Happiness
Gender	−0.18	−0.04
Marital status		
Divorced	−0.09	−0.02
Married	0.01	0.04
Single	(omitted)	(omitted)
Employment status		
Unemployed	(omitted)	(omitted)
Employed	−0.16	−0.05
Out of labor market	−0.20	−0.03
Income scale	0.16***	0.02
Importance of work	−0.14	−0.05*
Freedom of choice	0.51***	0.04***
Educational level	0.03	0.03*
Age	0.01	−0.01
Age squared	−0.00	0.00
Government's responsibility	−0.00	0.01
Satisfaction with politics	0.17***	0.02*
Constant (_cons)	1.47*	2.72***
N	950	950
R^2	0.42	0.07

*Legend * P < 0.05; ** P < 0.01; *** P < 0.001*

satisfaction, aligning with the observed positive effect in the data (Inglehart, 2020) (Table 3.4).

The R-squared value of 0.07 indicates that the model explains approximately 6.70% of the variance in the dependent variable.

The findings from Waves 6 and 7 provide a nuanced picture of the factors affecting life satisfaction and happiness in Kazakhstan. The comparison of factors affecting subjective well-being in Kazakhstan reveals both enduring patterns and significant evolutions in life satisfaction and happiness. Economic factors demonstrate remarkable consistency, with income maintaining a stable, positive relationship with life satisfaction ($\beta = 0.18$*** and $\beta = 0.16$*** across waves) while showing minimal impact on happiness—a finding that aligns with the Easterlin Paradox and suggests money improves life evaluation more than emotional well-being. The persistent importance of freedom of choice ($\beta = 0.27$*** to $\beta = 0.51$*** for life satisfaction) underscores autonomy as a fundamental psychological need across periods. The dramatic weakening of divorce's negative effect (from $\beta = -0.61$*** to $\beta = -0.09$) signals evolving social attitudes, while the fading benefit of marriage may reflect changing family dynamics in Kazakh society. Perhaps most significantly, political satisfaction emerges as a new predictor in later data ($\beta = 0.17$*** for life satisfaction), suggesting growing relevance of governance quality as the country develops. The diminishing impact of income equality and unemployment penalties hints at structural economic changes, possibly including improved social safety nets or labor market adjustments. The significant positive impacts of income, freedom of choice, and satisfaction with political performance on life satisfaction align with the literature, which emphasizes the importance of economic and personal autonomy in enhancing well-being. Conversely, the negative impacts of being divorced or unemployed on life satisfaction and happiness reflect well-documented consequences of socioeconomic challenges.

This comprehensive analysis reinforces the importance of addressing socioeconomic inequalities, ensuring job satisfaction, and fostering a supportive political environment to improve well-being. The insights gained from these data offer valuable guidance for policymakers and researchers aiming to enhance quality of life in Kazakhstan and similar contexts.

3.2 Economic Instability and Subjective Well-Being in Kyrgyzstan

Economic instability presents a significant challenge for developing countries, as it impacts various facets of life, including subjective well-being. In Kyrgyzstan, a country characterized by its complex economic landscape and historical transitions, the relationship between economic instability and individual well-being is particularly prominent. This chapter explores how economic fluctuations affect subjective well-being in Kyrgyzstan, drawing from empirical data, theoretical perspectives, and case studies, to provide a comprehensive analysis of this dynamic interaction.

The financial satisfaction score increased from 5.80 in Wave 4 to 6.38 in Wave 6. This represents an improvement in individuals' satisfaction with their financial situation over the time period between the two waves. The score increased by approximately 0.577, indicating a notable improvement in financial satisfaction (Fig. 3.1 and Table 3.5).

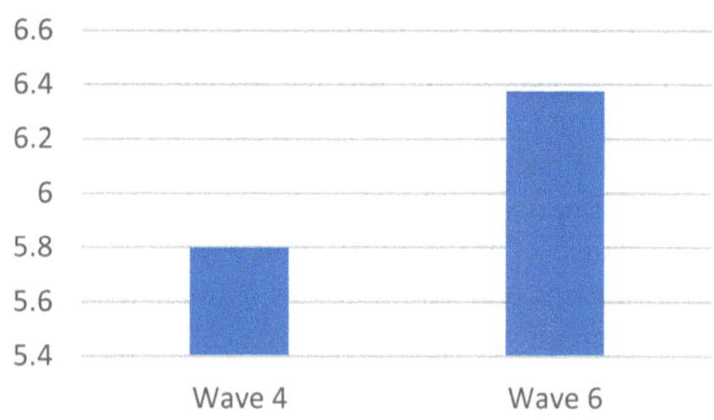

Fig. 3.1 Financial Satisfaction in Kyrgyzstan. *Source* World Values Survey (2024)

Table 3.5 Variable definitions

Variable	Definition
Life satisfaction	Measures overall satisfaction with life, where respondents rate their satisfaction from 1 (completely dissatisfied) to 10 (completely satisfied)
Happiness	Assesses overall happiness, where respondents rate their happiness from 1 (not at all happy) to 4 (very happy)
Age	The respondent's age in years
Age squared	The square of the respondent's age, calculated by multiplying the age by itself
Gender	Indicates the respondent's gender, where 0 typically represents female and 1 represents male
Educational level	Represents the highest level of education attained by the respondent, ranging from early childhood education (0) to the highest educational level achieved
Freedom of choice	Measures the level of freedom and control the respondent feels they have, rated from 1 (no choice at all) to 10 (the highest level of freedom)
Importance of work	Reflects how important work is in the respondent's life, rated from 1 (very important) to 4 (not at all important)
Income scale	Indicates the respondent's household income level on a scale from 1 (lowest income group) to 10 (highest income group) in their country
Employment status	Represents employment status through dummy variables. Categories include: Out of Labor Market (e.g., retired, homemaker, student), Unemployed (actively seeking employment), and Employed (full-time, part-time, or self-employed

The mean income equality in Wave 6 was approximately 6.12 with a standard deviation of approximately 2.96, and in Wave 4, it was approximately 5.44 with a standard deviation of approximately 3.02.

Regarding marital status, in Wave 6, the mean for being married was approximately 76.17% with a standard deviation of approximately 42.62% (Table 3.6).

A higher educational level is associated with a significant decrease in happiness in Wave 4. This could indicate that in this period, higher education might be correlated with factors that decrease happiness, such as higher expectations or job market pressures. Greater perceived freedom of choice significantly increases happiness. This aligns with the idea that personal freedom is strongly associated with increased well-being. Perceived freedom of choice has a strong positive effect on life satisfaction, indicating that the sense of autonomy is crucial for overall life satisfaction. Higher income scale positively affects life satisfaction, suggesting that financial resources are important for life satisfaction in Wave 4. A higher income scale has a significant positive effect on both happiness and life satisfaction in Wave 6. Unemployment has a positive but modest effect on happiness compared to being out of the labor market. People who support that husband and wife should both contribute to the income are less happy with their lives. Variable income equality significantly increases happiness in Wave 4, indicating that larger income equality has a positive effect on happiness. Being married significantly increases happiness and life satisfaction. Being single also has a positive effect on happiness, though less pronounced

Table 3.6 Descriptive statistics

Variable	Wave 6		Wave 4		Min	Max
	Mean	Std. Dev	Mean	Std. Dev		
Happiness	3.32	0.56	3.07	0.59	1	4
Life satisfaction	6.96	2.16	6.64	2.48	1	10
Age	38.73	14.39	36.51	15.03	18	89
Age Squared	1707.14	1250.88	1558.37	1337.93	324	7921
Educational Level	6.80	1.93	6.72	1.93	1	9
Freedom of Choice	7.38	2.21	7.15	2.44	1	10
Importance of Work	1.44	0.67	1.53	0.71	1	4
Income Scale	5.56	2.06	4.35	1.36	1	10
Out of Labor Market	0.35	0.48	0.34	0.47	0	1
Unemployed	0.11	0.31	0.19	0.39	0	1
Employed	0.55	0.50	0.47	0.50	0	1
Income Equality	6.12	2.96	5.44	3.02	1	10
Gender	0.49	0.50			0	1
Married	0.76	0.43			0	1
Single	0.15	0.36			0	1
Divorced	0.09	0.28			0	1
Husband and Wife Contribute			1.98	0.85	1	4
N	1452		854			

compared to being married. Being single has an even stronger positive effect on life satisfaction compared to being married in Wave 6 (Table 3.7).

This chapter investigates the intricate relationship between economic instability and subjective well-being in Kyrgyzstan via empirical data from Waves 4 and 6. The analysis highlights several key findings about how economic and sociodemographic variables influence individuals' happiness and life satisfaction. These findings are juxtaposed with literature to provide a nuanced understanding of the dynamics at play in Kyrgyzstan. The comparison between Wave 4 and Wave 6 data reveals significant shifts in how economic factors influence subjective well-being in Kyrgyzstan. While income maintains its importance for life satisfaction with a strengthening effect ($\beta = 0.13^*$ to $\beta = 0.24^*$), its minimal impact on happiness persists, reinforcing the Easterlin Paradox. The most striking change appears in employment dynamics: unemployment transitions from having neutral/negative associations in Wave 4 to showing positive correlations with both happiness ($\beta = 0.12^*$) and life satisfaction ($\beta = 0.23$) in Wave 6, potentially reflecting the growing role of informal economies or strengthened social safety nets. Freedom of choice remains significant, though diminished in effect size ($\beta = 0.48^*$ to $\beta = 0.19^{***}$ for life satisfaction), while education loses its previously negative association with well-being. Wave 6 introduces marital status as a strong predictor (married $\beta = 0.66^{**}$ for life satisfaction) and reveals emerging

Table 3.7 Economic factors affecting to subjective well-being in Kyrgyzstan

Variable	Wave 4		Wave 6	
	Happiness	Life satisfaction	Happiness	Life satisfaction
Age	−0.00	−0.02	−0.02**	−0.02
Age squared	0.00	0.00	0.00*	0.00
Educational level	−0.05***	−0.10*	−0.01	0.02
Choice of freedom	0.04***	0.48***	0.02**	0.19***
Importance of work	0.01	0.09	−0.02	−0.10
Income scale	0.02	0.13*	0.02*	0.24***
Employment				
Out of labor market	(omitted)	(omitted)	(omitted)	(omitted)
Unemployed	−0.09	−0.17	0.12*	0.23
Employed	0.01	−0.21	0.05	0.21
Husband and wife contribute	−0.00	0.24**		
Income equality	0.03***	0.00	−0.00	0.01
Gender			−0.02	−0.23
Married			0.30***	0.66**
Single			0.18*	0.90***
Divorced	(omitted)	(omitted)	(omitted)	(omitted)
Constant (_cons)	3.08***	3.65***	3.27***	3.79***
N	854	854	1452	1452
R^2	0.08	0.28	0.05	0.11

*Legend * P < 0.05; ** P < 0.01; *** P < 0.001*

gender disparities (female $\beta = -0.23$ for life satisfaction). These changes suggest Kyrgyzstan's well-being landscape is undergoing transformation, where traditional economic indicators interact with evolving social structures and cultural values.

The findings from Kyrgyzstan echo several themes prevalent in the literature on subjective well-being. For instance, the positive impact of financial satisfaction and income on life satisfaction aligns with the economic literature emphasizing the importance of financial stability for well-being (Diener et al., 2018). The role of freedom of choice and autonomy as crucial determinants of well-being is consistently supported by self-determination theory (Deci & Ryan, 2012).

The nuanced relationship between age, education, and well-being observed in Kyrgyzstan reflects broader trends noted in the literature, where age and education have complex effects on happiness and life satisfaction (Blanchflower & Oswald, 2008; Helliwell & Huang, 2008). Additionally, the varying impact of income equality over time in Kyrgyzstan is consistent with studies suggesting that while income equality can enhance well-being, its impact may be moderated by other economic factors (Wilkinson & Pickett, 2009).

In summary, the analysis of economic instability and subjective well-being in Kyrgyzstan reveals a multifaceted relationship influenced by various economic and sociodemographic factors. The findings emphasize the importance of economic stability, freedom of choice, and social factors in shaping individual well-being. Future research should continue to explore these dynamics, considering the interplay of economic fluctuations, policy interventions, and sociocultural changes in developing countries.

3.2.1 Economic Factors of Happiness in Tajikistan

This chapter explores how economic factors, social dynamics, and cultural influences shape the subjective well-being of Tajikistan's population. Despite its challenges, including economic fluctuations and sociopolitical changes, Tajikistan offers insights into the complex relationship between economic development and happiness. By examining various facets of life in Tajikistan—from income levels and employment opportunities to social cohesion and mental health—we aim to provide a comprehensive analysis of what contributes to happiness in this diverse and resilient nation.

Tajikistan's economy has undergone significant transformations since gaining independence from the Soviet Union in 1991. Initially, grappling with the transition to a market economy, Tajikistan faced economic hardships, exacerbated by civil war in the 1990s. However, in recent years, the country has shown signs of economic growth, largely driven by remittances from Tajik migrant workers abroad, particularly in Russia. This section investigates key economic indicators such as GDP per capita, inflation rates, and employment patterns, examining their impact on the well-being and happiness of Tajik citizens. Despite economic growth, disparities in income distribution and access to basic services remain significant challenges that influence overall happiness levels. Studies such as those by Kim (2023) find a positive but modest relationship between economic growth and happiness in Tajikistan. While increases in GDP per capita are associated with higher levels of happiness, the effect is not as pronounced as it is in more developed economies. Borisova (2024) examine the complexities of migration in Tajikistan and its impact on well-being and perceptions of a "good life." The transition from a centrally planned economy to a market-oriented system in Tajikistan has led to significant changes in economic conditions and individual well-being. While economic growth has generally improved living standards, its impact on happiness is complex and multifaceted (Guriev & Melnikov, 2018).

Yamada et al. (2022) estimated remittances and household welfare and reported that the effect of remittances on household spending is more pronounced in households with male, older, or less educated heads. This study provides valuable evidence on the impact of the COVID-19 pandemic on migration and household welfare in Tajikistan, a country heavily reliant on remittance inflows, particularly from Russia.

Tokhirov (2023) revealed that exposure to income shocks, such as the 2010/11 world cotton price increase, negatively impacts households' satisfaction with their lives and financial situations. Interestingly, while remittances can help mitigate some negative effects on financial satisfaction, they do not significantly improve overall life satisfaction. This highlights the complexity of subjective well-being, suggesting that distinctions should be made between different domains of well-being, such as general and financial satisfaction.

This chapter investigates the intricate relationship between economic factors and subjective well-being in Tajikistan, a nation marked by significant economic and social transitions. My analysis draws on recent data from the World Values Survey (WVS) and integrates findings from various studies to provide a comprehensive overview of how economic and social conditions shape happiness and life satisfaction in Central Asian countries.

The World Values Survey (WVS) is a global research project that examines socio-cultural and political values across various countries in waves. Each wave represents a specific round of data collection, focusing on the attitudes, beliefs, and values of individuals within different societies. I used the data from WVS for the 7th wave collected for Tajikistan in 2020 (Table 3.8).

This table presents descriptive statistics summarizing data collected from a representative sample of Tajikistan's population. On average, respondents rate their life satisfaction at approximately 7.93, with a range from 1 (minimum) to 10 (maximum). The standard deviation of 1.85 indicates the variability in life satisfaction scores among the respondents. The average happiness score is 3.56, with scores ranging from 1 to 4. The standard deviation of 0.61 suggests relatively low variability in happiness

Table 3.8 Variable definitions

Variable	Definition
Life satisfaction	Overall satisfaction with life, rated from 1 (completely dissatisfied) to 10 (completely satisfied)
Happiness	General happiness level, rated from 1 (not at all happy) to 4 (very happy)
Age	The respondent's age in years
Age squared	The square of the respondent's age, calculated by multiplying the age by itself
Gender	Indicates the respondent's gender, where 0 represents female and 1 represents male
Married, single, divorced	Represents marital status as a set of dummy variables. Each status (married, single, divorced) is coded as 1 or 0
Out of labor, unemployed employed	Employment status is represented by a set of dummy variables. Categories include: Out of Labor Market (retired/pensioned, homemaker, student), Unemployed (actively seeking employment), and Employed (full-time, part-time, or self-employed)
Health status	State of health (subjective) indicates (1) very good to (5) very poor
Financial satisfaction	Satisfaction with financial situation of household where (1) completely dissatisfied to (10) completely satisfied

ratings among respondents. The average age of the respondents was 44.23 years, with ages ranging from 18–83 years. The standard deviation of 13.68 indicates moderate variability in age among respondents. Age squared is often used in regression analyses to capture nonlinear relationships with age. Gender is coded as binary (0 for female, 1 for male). The mean of 0.49 suggests a nearly equal distribution between genders, with a standard deviation of 0.50 indicating equal variability. The marital status category indicates that 94.23% of the respondents are married, 0.31% are single, and 5.46% are divorced. The employment status category indicates that 45.33% of the respondents are employed, 29.91% are out of labor, and 24.76% are unemployed. The average health status rating is 2.09, with ratings ranging from 1 (poor health) to 5 (excellent health). The standard deviation of 0.83 indicates variability in health status among respondents. On average, respondents rate their financial satisfaction at 7.03, with ratings ranging from 1 (very dissatisfied) to 10 (very satisfied). The standard deviation of 1.97 indicates variability in financial satisfaction among respondents. The total number of respondents in the dataset is 953 (Table 3.9).

This table explores various socioeconomic factors that contribute to subjective well-being, reflecting the complex interplay between individual perceptions of happiness and broader socioeconomic conditions. These factors encompass economic indicators and social dynamics that shape individuals' subjective assessments of their overall life satisfaction and happiness levels (Table 3.10).

Being single has a statistically significant positive effect on happiness, with a coefficient of 0.55. Compared with individuals with other marital statuses, single

Table 3.9 Descriptive Statistics

Variable	Mean	Std. Dev	Min	Max
Life satisfaction	7.93	1.85	1	10
Happiness	3.56	0.61	1	4
Age	44.23	13.68	18	83
Age squared	2142.84	1283.33	324	6889
Gender	0.49	0.50	0	1
Marital status				
Married	0.94	0.23	0	1
Single	0.00	0.06	0	1
Divorced	0.05	0.23	0	1
Employment status				
Out of labor market	0.30	0.46	0	1
Unemployed	0.25	0.43	0	1
Employed	0.45	0.50	0	1
Health status	2.09	0.83	1	5
Financial satisfaction	7.03	1.97	1	10
Observations (Obs)	953			

Table 3.10 Socioeconomic factors of subjective well-being in Tajikistan

Variable	Happiness	Life satisfaction
Age	0.00	0.05*
Age Squared	0.00	−0.00
Gender	−0.02	0.04
Marital status		
Married	0.22	0.58*
Single	0.55**	1.42*
Divorced	(omitted)	(omitted)
Employment status		
Out of Labor Market	0.01	0.14
Unemployed	(omitted)	(omitted)
Employed	−0.01	0.17
Health Status	−0.19***	−0.12
Financial Satisfaction	0.07***	0.52***
Constant (_cons)	3.17***	2.64***
N	953	953
R^2	0.15	0.33

Legend * $p < 0.05$; ** $p < 0.01$; *** $p < 0.001$

individuals tend to report higher levels of happiness. Health status has a statistically significant negative effect on happiness, with a coefficient of −0.19. This suggests that individuals with poorer health tend to report lower levels of happiness. This finding supports the findings of previous studies (Diener & Chan, 2011). Financial satisfaction has a statistically significant and strong positive effect on happiness, with a coefficient of 0.07. This finding indicates that individuals who are more satisfied with their financial situation tend to report higher levels of happiness. Employment status, gender, age and age squared have statistically insignificant results.

The results for life satisfaction indicate that age has a statistically significant positive effect on life satisfaction, with a coefficient of 0.05. This suggests that as individuals grow older, their reported levels of life satisfaction tend to increase. Being married also has a statistically significant positive effect on life satisfaction, with a coefficient of 0.57, although the effect is smaller than that of being single (1.41). These findings support previous findings that marriage typically contributes positively to life satisfaction through various mechanisms, including emotional support and shared resources (Waite & Gallagher, 2001). Financial satisfaction has a statistically significant positive effect on life satisfaction, with a coefficient of 0.52. This finding indicates that individuals who are more satisfied with their financial situation tend to report higher levels of life satisfaction.

The analysis presented in this chapter emphasizes the complex interplay between economic factors and subjective well-being in Tajikistan. While economic growth and financial satisfaction play crucial roles in enhancing happiness, other factors, such as health status, employment quality, and social support, also significantly impact well-being. Addressing these multifaceted issues through targeted policies can contribute to improved happiness and life satisfaction in Tajikistan. By understanding and addressing the diverse factors that shape well-being, Tajikistan can work toward fostering a more resilient and content society.

On the basis of these findings, several policy implications can be drawn for enhancing subjective well-being in Tajikistan:

1. Policies should focus on promoting equitable economic growth and reducing income inequality to improve overall well-being. Ensuring that the benefits of economic growth are distributed more evenly can help mitigate the negative effects of income disparities on happiness.
2. Strengthening financial security and improving access to economic opportunities can enhance financial satisfaction and, consequently, happiness. This includes supporting job creation, providing social safety nets, and improving access to financial services.
3. Improving the quality and stability of employment is crucial. Policies should aim to provide stable job opportunities and enhance job satisfaction to positively impact happiness.
4. Investing in healthcare infrastructure and services is essential for improving health outcomes and, by extension, happiness. Addressing health disparities and ensuring access to quality healthcare can have a significant impact on subjective well-being.

3.2.2 Income and Life Satisfaction in Uzbekistan

This chapter examines the intersection of happiness and economics in Uzbekistan, exploring how economic policies, social changes, and cultural factors influence the well-being of its people (Table 3.11).

The mean happiness score of 3.63 on a scale from 1 to 4 suggests a moderately positive outlook among respondents. The standard deviation of 0.55 indicates variability in happiness levels. The average life satisfaction score is 7.93 out of 10, with a standard deviation of 1.82. The average age of the respondents is 39.50 years, with a standard deviation of 14.51, suggesting a broad age range from 18–89 years. The quadratic term of age (age squared) has a mean of 1770.55, which is used to capture the potential nonlinear relationship between age and well-being. This suggests that the impact of age on happiness or life satisfaction may change as individuals grow older. The respondents reported a mean financial satisfaction score of 3.99 on a scale from 1–10, with a standard deviation of 2.02. The mean score for income equality is 4.61, with a standard deviation of 3.12. The average education level is 5.90 on a scale from 1–9, with a standard deviation of 1.46. The mean score for freedom of choice is 7.91, with a standard deviation of 2.30. Approximately 43.30% of the respondents did not actively participate in the labor force. A total of 13.75% of the sample reported being unemployed, and 42.96% of the respondents were employed,

Table 3.11 Variable definitions

Variable	Definition
Life satisfaction	Overall satisfaction with life, where 1 = completely dissatisfied and 10 = completely satisfied
Happiness	Self-reported happiness level, where 1 = not at all happy, 2 = not very happy, 3 = rather happy, and 4 = very happy
Age	Age of the respondent in years
Age squared	The square of the respondent's age (age * age)
Financial satisfaction	Satisfaction with household financial situation, where 1 = completely dissatisfied and 10 = completely satisfied
Income equality	Opinion on income equality, where 1 = incomes should be made more equal and 10 = incomes should not be made more equal
Education level	Highest level of education achieved, from early childhood education (0) to the highest level attained
Freedom of choice	Perceived freedom of choice and control, where 1 = no choice at all and 10 = the highest level of freedom
Importance of work	Importance of work in life, where 1 = very important and 4 = not at all important
Income scale	Household income level on a scale from 1 to 10, where 1 = lowest income group and 10 = highest income group
Single	Marital status dummy variable: 1 if single, 0 otherwise
Married	Marital status dummy variable: 1 if married, 0 otherwise
Divorced	Marital status dummy variable: 1 if divorced, 0 otherwise
Unemployed	Employment status dummy variable: 1 if unemployed (actively seeking employment), 0 otherwise
Employed	Employment status dummy variable: 1 if employed (full-time, part-time, or self-employed), 0 otherwise
Out of labor market	Employment status dummy variable: 1 if out of the labor market (retired, homemaker, or student), 0 otherwise
Health status	Subjective state of health, where 1 = very good and 5 = very poor
Gender	Gender of the respondent: 0 = female, 1 = male

reflecting a relatively high level of participation in the labor market. The majority of the respondents (75.17%) were married, 13.23% were single, and 11.60% were divorced. The mean health status score is 2.04, with a standard deviation of 0.79 on a scale from 1 to 4. The variable "Important: Work" measures the significance that respondents place on their work, with a mean score of 1.43 on a scale from 1 to 4, where 4 represents the least importance and 1 represents the highest importance.

The income scale measures respondents' perceptions of their income level, with a mean score of 5.91 on a scale from 1 to 10, where 1 represents the lowest income level and 10 represents the highest income level (Table 3.12).

The coefficient for age squared is small, but statistically significant. This positive coefficient implies a U-shaped relationship between age and life satisfaction. The

Table 3.12 Descriptive statistics

Variable	Mean	Std. Dev	Min	Max
Happiness	3.63	0.55	1	4
Life satisfaction	7.93	1.82	1	10
Age	39.50	14.51	18	89
Age Sqr	1770.55	1304.69	324	7921
Financial satisfaction	3.99	2.02	1	10
Income equality	4.61	3.12	1	10
Education level	5.90	1.46	1	9
Freedom of choice	7.91	2.30	1	10
Important: work	1.43	0.82	1	4
Income scale	5.91	1.75	1	10
Out of labor market	0.43	0.50	0	1
Unemployed	0.14	0.34	0	1
Employed	0.43	0.50	0	1
Gender	0.41	0.49	0	1
Married	0.75	0.43	0	1
Single	0.13	0.34	0	1
Divorced	0.12	0.32	0	1
Health status	2.04	0.79	1	4
N	1164			

substantial negative coefficient indicates that greater financial satisfaction is associated with lower life satisfaction (−0.38, significant at the 1% level). This counterintuitive result may reflect the complex relationship between financial resources and overall life satisfaction, potentially influenced by other factors such as expectations, social comparisons, or psychological adaptation. The positive coefficient indicates that greater perceived income equality contributes to higher life satisfaction. The lack of significance implies that variations in education level do not strongly affect life satisfaction in this context. This suggests that, at least in this sample, education level does not have a direct or substantial effect on overall life satisfaction and happiness. Freedom of choice, employment status, gender, and marital status did not significantly influence life satisfaction in this sample.

This negative coefficient suggests that placing greater importance on work is associated with high life satisfaction. This positive relationship indicates that higher perceived income levels are associated with greater life satisfaction. This finding supports the general idea that improved economic conditions contribute to increased life satisfaction. A positive relationship between income scale and life satisfaction indicates that higher perceived income levels are associated with greater life satisfaction. A strong negative relationship indicates that poorer health is associated with greater life satisfaction. The R-squared value of 0.32 indicates that approximately

32.5% of the variability in life satisfaction is explained by the model. This suggests that the model captures a significant portion of the variability in life satisfaction.

The coefficient for age is −0.02, indicating a small but significant negative effect of age on happiness. Older individuals report slightly lower levels of happiness, although the effect size is modest. Similar to life satisfaction, this positive coefficient suggests that the U-shaped impact of age on happiness diminishes as people continue to age. Contrary to the literature, the negative relationship suggests that financial satisfaction is associated with lower happiness. This implies that financial satisfaction alone might not be a strong predictor of happiness and may interact with other variables. The negative impact of valuing work highly on happiness suggests that those who prioritize work might experience greater happiness. Being married is strongly associated with greater happiness (0.39, significant at the 1% level). This emphasizes the positive impact of marital status on well-being, potentially due to social support and companionship. Poorer health is also associated with lower happiness, emphasizing the substantial impact of health on overall well-being (−0.14, significant at the 1% level) (Table 3.13).

The R-squared value of 0.18 indicates that approximately 18.1% of the variability in happiness is explained by the model. This lower R-squared value suggests that

Table 3.13 Factors affecting subjective well-being in Uzbekistan

Variable	Life satisfaction	Happiness
Age	−0.04	−0.02*
Age sqr	0.00*	0.00**
Financial satisfaction	−0.38***	−0.05***
Income equality	0.05***	−0.00
Education level	−0.05	−0.01
Freedom of choice	0.03	0.01
Important: work	−0.15*	−0.10***
Income scale	0.08*	−0.01
Out of labor market	(omitted)	(omitted)
Unemployed	−0.13	−0.02
Employed	−0.21	−0.04
Income equality	(omitted)	(omitted)
Gender	0.04	−0.03
Married	0.31	0.39***
Single	0.18	0.14
Divorced	(omitted)	(omitted)
Health status	−0.39***	−0.14***
cons	10.44***	4.37***
N	1164	1164
r^2	0.32	0.18

*Legend * p < 0.05; ** p < 0.01; *** p < 0.001*

happiness is influenced by a broader range of factors and that the model may not fully capture all relevant determinants of happiness.

The findings from Uzbekistan both align with and diverge from the literature on subjective well-being. The positive relationship between income scale scores and life satisfaction is consistent with studies demonstrating that financial resources can enhance life satisfaction (Diener & Seligman, 2004). However, the negative effect of financial satisfaction on life satisfaction and happiness introduces complexity into the understanding of financial well-being, suggesting that other factors, such as expectations or social comparisons, might play a role (Easterlin, 2001).

The U-shaped relationship between age and life satisfaction aligns with the U-shaped age–happiness curve observed in other studies (Blanchflower & Oswald, 2008). This finding suggests that while age may initially be associated with declining well-being, it may improve in later years. The lack of a significant impact of education level on life satisfaction contrasts with broader literature suggesting a positive relationship, indicating that the effects of education on well-being may vary on the basis of context and other influencing factors.

The limited impact of freedom of choice and employment status on life satisfaction in Uzbekistan suggests that cultural and contextual factors may influence how these variables are perceived and valued, differing from general findings in other regions (Clark et al., 2017; Deci & Ryan, 2012). The strong positive impact of marriage on well-being is consistent with extensive literature highlighting the benefits of marital relationships (Kalmijn, 2005). The significant impact of health on well-being emphasizes the crucial role of health in determining subjective well-being, which is consistent with broader research (Marmot & Bobak, 2005).

In summary, this chapter provides a nuanced view of how income and other sociodemographic factors influence life satisfaction and happiness in Uzbekistan. The findings emphasize the complex interplay between economic resources, personal expectations, and contextual factors in shaping subjective well-being. Future research should continue to explore these dynamics, considering the broader socioeconomic and cultural context to provide a more comprehensive understanding of well-being in Uzbekistan and similar settings.

3.3 Conclusion

In conclusion, the dynamics between economic development and happiness in Central Asia are complex and multifaceted. The study has shed light on the various influences on well-being in the region, including the impacts of economic growth, income inequality, social policies, and cultural factors. It is evident that while economic growth can lead to improvements in living standards and access to essential services, it does not always directly translate into increased happiness, especially in the presence of significant disparities in income and opportunities. The findings emphasize the importance of tailored economic and social policies aimed at enhancing overall well-being. The findings present intriguing parallels to and divergences from the Easterlin Paradox, which posits that while higher income correlates with greater happiness at a point in time, long-term economic growth does not necessarily lead to higher aggregate happiness (Easterlin, 1974). The strong cross-sectional relationship between financial satisfaction and life satisfaction in Tajikistan ($\beta = 0.52$, $p < 0.001$) and Kyrgyzstan (Wave 4: $\beta = 0.48$, $p < 0.001$) initially appears to support the within-country dimension of the paradox. However, the weakening of this association in Kyrgyzstan's later wave (Wave 6: $\beta = 0.19$, $p < 0.001$) suggests a potential dynamic consistent with Easterlin's longitudinal observations—as economic development progresses, the marginal utility of additional income may diminish in its capacity to enhance well-being. The paradoxical finding that unemployment in Kyrgyzstan correlates with higher happiness ($\beta = 0.12$, $p < 0.05$) may represent an extreme case of the Easterlin Paradox mechanisms, where social comparisons and adaptation processes outweigh absolute material conditions. In this context, the prevalence of informal employment and strong community support networks may mitigate the psychological impact of formal unemployment, while simultaneously reducing the aspirational comparisons that typically drive the income-happiness relationship in more marketized economies. This aligns with Easterlin's later work emphasizing the role of social norms and comparisons in mediating economic effects on well-being (Easterlin, 2001). The marital status findings offer additional insights into the Paradox's social dimension. While marriage enhances happiness in Uzbekistan ($\beta = 0.39$, $p < 0.001$) and Tajikistan ($\beta = 0.22$), the strong negative effect of divorce in Kazakhstan ($\beta = -0.61$, $p < 0.001$) suggests that social and familial bonds may serve as alternative sources of well-being when economic growth plateaus—a phenomenon observed in Western nations where social connectedness often outweighs material factors in long-term happiness (Helliwell et al., 2019).

The U-shaped age pattern in Uzbekistan, combined with the marital status findings, suggests that life course happiness may be less tied to economic factors than to culturally specific social roles and expectations—an important qualifier to Easterlin's primarily economic paradox. These results collectively suggest that while the Easterlin Paradox provides a valuable framework for understanding Central Asian SWB dynamics, its mechanisms operate differently in these transitioning, collectivist societies compared to the Western contexts where it was originally formulated. The role of informal economies, the strength of familial networks, and the pace of value change all appear to mediate how economic factors translate into subjective well-being in ways that both confirm and challenge the Paradox's predictions.

Future research should explicitly test Easterlin's hypotheses in these contexts, particularly examining whether: (1) the income-happiness gradient flattens at lower absolute income levels than in the West, (2) social comparisons operate more within extended family networks than at societal levels, and (3) adaptation to improved circumstances occurs more slowly in these cultural contexts. Such investigations could both refine the Paradox's cross-cultural applicability and generate new insights about well-being in transitional economies.

Moving forward, policymakers in Central Asia can use the insights from this study to inform the design and implementation of effective strategies that prioritize well-being alongside economic development. By doing so, they can work toward creating more balanced and inclusive societies where economic progress aligns with increased happiness and life satisfaction for all individuals.

References

Abdur Rahman, A., & Veenhoven, R. (2018). Freedom and Happiness in Nations: A Research Synthesis. *Applied Research in Quality of Life,* 13(2), 435–456.

Alkire, S. (2005). Subjective Quantitative Studies of Human Agency. *Social Indicators Research, 74*(1), 217–260. https://doi.org/10.1007/s11205-005-6525-0

Analytical Tables—Agency on Statistics Under the President of the Republic of Tajikistan. (2023). *Агентии омори назди Президенти Ҷумҳурии Тоҷикистон* (blog). https://www.stat.tj/en/analytical-tables/

Anand, P., Hunter, G., & Smith, R. (2005). Capabilities and Well-Being: Evidence Based on the Sen-Nussbaum Approach to Welfare. *Social Indicators Research, 74*(1), 9–55. https://doi.org/10.1007/s11205-005-6518-z

Bartolini, S., Mikucka, M., & Sarracino, F. (2017). Money, Trust and Happiness in Transition Countries: Evidence from Time Series. *Social Indicators Research, 130*(1), 87–106. https://doi.org/10.1007/s11205-015-1130-3

Batsaikhan, U., & Dabrowski, M. (2017). Central Asia—Twenty-Five Years after the Breakup of the USSR. *Russian Journal of Economics, 3*(3), 296–320.

Bhuiyan, S. (2012). Political Leadership and Its Role in Achieving Good Governance in Kazakhstan. *International Journal of Public Administration, 35*(6), 379–388. https://doi.org/10.1080/01900692.2012.655525

Bian, Y., Hao, M., & Li, Y. (2018). Social Networks and Subjective Well-Being: A Comparison of Australia, Britain, and China. *Journal of Happiness Studies, 19*(8), 2489–2508. https://doi.org/10.1007/s10902-017-9926-2

Bjørnskov, C. (2003). The Happy Few: Cross-Country Evidence on Social Capital and Life Satisfaction. *Available at SSRN 381640.*

Bjørnskov, C. (2006). The Multiple Facets of Social Capital. *European Journal of Political Economy, 22*(1), 22–40.

Bjørnskov, C. (2008). Social Capital and Happiness in the United States. *Applied Research in Quality of Life, 3*, 43–62.

Blanchflower, D. G., & Oswald, A. J. (2008). Is Well-Being U-Shaped over the Life Cycle? *Social Science & Medicine, 66*(8), 1733–1749.

Borisova, E. (2024). *Paradoxes of Migration in Tajikistan: Locating the Good Life.* UCL Press. https://books.google.com/books?hl=en&lr=&id=S68FEQAAQBAJ&oi=fnd&pg=PP1&dq=Economic+factors+of+happiness+in+Tajikistan&ots=ptgWwZsRdp&sig=0EInHqxKn1pBlMJx71eLNZM1uZU

Brehm, J., & Rahn, W. (1997). Individual-Level Evidence for the Causes and Consequences of Social Capital. *American Journal of Political Science*, 999–1023.

Cheng, Z., & Smyth, R. (2015). Crime Victimization, Neighborhood Safety and Happiness in China. *Economic Modelling, 51*, 424–435.

Clark, A. E., Flèche, S., Layard, R., Powdthavee, N., & Ward, G. (2017). *The Key Determinants of Happiness and Misery.* https://eprints.lse.ac.uk/83622

Clark, A. E., Frijters, P. & Shields, M. A. (2006). *Income and Happiness: Evidence, Explanations and Economic Implications.* https://shs.hal.science/halshs-00590436/

Collins, K., & Gambrel, R. (2017). Corruption and Popular Support for Democracy and Government in Transitional Contexts: The Case of Kyrgyzstan. *Europe-Asia Studies, 69*(8), 1280–1309. https://doi.org/10.1080/09668136.2017.1384449

Cummings, S. N., & Ryabkov, M. (2013). Situating the 'Tulip Revolution.' In *Domestic and International Perspectives on Kyrgyzstan's 'Tulip Revolution,'* 19–30. Routledge. https://api.taylorfrancis.com/content/chapters/edit/download?identifierName=doi&identifierValue=10.4324/9781315876092-4&type=chapterpdf

Dadabaev, T. (2007). Trajectories of Political Development and Public Choices in Turkmenistan. *Asian Affairs: An American Review, 34*(3), 131–150. https://doi.org/10.3200/AAFS.34.3.131-150

Deci, E. L., & Ryan, R. M. (2012). Self-determination Theory. *Handbook of Theories of Social Psychology, 1*(20), 416–436.

Delhey, J., Hess, S., Boehnke, K., Deutsch, F., Eichhorn, J., Kühnen, U., & Welzel, C. (2023). Life Satisfaction During the COVID-19 Pandemic: The Role of Human, Economic, Social, and Psychological Capital. *Journal of Happiness Studies, 24*(7), 2201–2222.

Demircioglu, M. A., & Sharipova, D. (2023). Does Public Sector Employment Matter for Subjective Well-Being?: The Case of Kazakhstan. *International Journal of Public Administration*, 1–16.

Demografiya. (2024). *2024.* https://stat.uz/uz/rasmiy-statistika/demography-2

Diener, A. C. (2005). Kazakhstan's Kin State Diaspora: Settlement Planning and the Oralman Dilemma. *Europe-Asia Studies, 57*(2), 327–348. https://doi.org/10.1080/09668130500052005

Diener, Ed. (2000). Subjective Well-Being: The Science of Happiness and a Proposal for a National Index. *American Psychologist,* 55(1), 34.

Diener, Ed, & Biswas-Diener, R. 2002. Will Money Increase Subjective Well-Being? *Social Indicators Research,* 57(2), 119–169. https://doi.org/10.1023/A:1014411319119

Diener, Ed, & Chan, M. Y. (2011). Happy People Live Longer: Subjective Well-Being Contributes to Health and Longevity: HEALTH BENEFITS OF HAPPINESS. *Applied Psychology: Health and Well-Being,* 3(1), 1–43. https://doi.org/10.1111/j.1758-0854.2010.01045.x

Diener, E., Diener, C., Choi, H., & Oishi, S. (2018). Revisiting 'Most People Are Happy'—And Discovering When They Are Not. *Perspectives on Psychological Science,* 13(2), 166–170. https://doi.org/10.1177/1745691618765111

Diener, Ed, & Seligman, M. E. P. (2004). Beyond Money: Toward an Economy of Well-Being. *Psychological Science in the Public Interest, 5*(1), 1–31. https://doi.org/10.1111/j.0963-7214.2004.00501001.x

Diener, E., Suh, E. M., Lucas, R. E., & Smith, H. L. (1999). Subjective Well-Being: Three Decades of Progress. *Psychological Bulletin,* 125(2), 276.

Dolan, P., & Peasgood, T. (2008). Measuring Well-Being for Public Policy: Preferences or Experiences? *The Journal of Legal Studies, 37*(S2), S5-31. https://doi.org/10.1086/595676

Easterlin, R. A. (2001). Income and Happiness: Towards a Unified Theory. *The Economic Journal, 111*(473), 465–484. https://doi.org/10.1111/1468-0297.00646

Ekici, T., & Koydemir, S. (2014). Social Capital, Government and Democracy Satisfaction, and Happiness in Turkey: A Comparison of Surveys in 1999 and 2008. *Social Indicators Research, 118*, 1031–1053.

Falkingham, J. (2000). *Women and Gender Relations in Tajikistan.* Asian Development Bank, Programs Department East and Office of Environment … https://www.adb.org/sites/default/files/institutional-document/32601/women-tajikistan.pdf

Flavin, P., & Keane, M. J. (2012). Life Satisfaction and Political Participation: Evidence from the United States. *Journal of Happiness Studies, 13*(1), 63–78. https://doi.org/10.1007/s10902-011-9250-1

Gauntlett, D. (2018). *Making Is Connecting: The Social Power of Creativity, from Craft and Knitting to Digital Everything*. John Wiley & Sons. https://books.google.com/books?hl=en&lr=&id=VpNcDwAAQBAJ&oi=fnd&pg=PT7&dq=David+Gauntlett,+Making+Is+Connecting:+The+Social+Power+of+Creativity,+from+Craft+and+Knitting+to+Digital+Everything+(John+Wiley+%26+Sons,+2018),+&ots=3Mx4MbWysD&sig=9AfqvnDp_0FrDa5tRY9LWtUrKa8

Graham, C. (2008). Happiness and Health: Lessons—And Questions—For Public Policy. *Health Affairs, 27*(1), 72–87. https://doi.org/10.1377/hlthaff.27.1.72

Growiec, K., & Growiec, J. (2014). Trusting Only Whom You Know, Knowing Only Whom You Trust: The Joint Impact of Social Capital and Trust on Happiness in CEE Countries. *Journal of Happiness Studies, 15*(5), 1015–1040. https://doi.org/10.1007/s10902-013-9461-8

Gullette, D. (2010). Institutionalized Instability: Factors Leading to the April 2010 Uprising in Kyrgyzstan. *Eurasian Review, 3*, 89–105.

Guriev, S., & Melnikov, N. (2018). Happiness Convergence in Transition Countries. *Journal of Comparative Economics, 46*(3), 683–707.

Haerpfer, C., Inglehart, R., Moreno, A., Welzel, C., Kizilova, K., Diez-Medrano J., M. Lagos, P. Norris, E. Ponarin & B. Puranen et al. (eds.). (2020). *World Values Survey: Round Seven Country-Pooled Datafile*. Madrid, Spain & Vienna, Austria: JD Systems Institute & WVSA Secretariat. https://doi.org/10.14281/18241.1

Hagerty, M. R., & Veenhoven, R. (2003). Wealth and Happiness Revisited-Growing National Income Does Go with Greater Happiness. *Social Indicators Research, 64*, 1–27.

Harris, C. (2000). The Changing Identity of Women in Tajikistan in the Post-Soviet Period. In Acar, F., & Ayse G. (Ed.), *InGender and Identity Construction: Women of Central Asia, the Caucasus, and Turkey*. https://brill.com/downloadpdf/display/book/edcoll/9789004492028/B9789004492028_s013.pdf

Helliwell, J. F., & Huang, H. (2008). How's Your Government? International Evidence Linking Good Government and Well-Being. *British Journal of Political Science, 38*(4), 595–619.

Helliwell, J. F., & Putnam, R. D. (2004). The Social Context of Well–Being. In F. A. Huppert, N. Baylis, & B. Keverne (Eds.), *Philosophical Transactions of the Royal Society of London. Series B: Biological Sciences*, 359(1449), 1435–1446. https://doi.org/10.1098/rstb.2004.1522

Hofstede, G. (2001). *Culture's Consequences: Comparing Values, Behaviors, Institutions and Organizations across Nations*. Sage publications. https://books.google.com/books?hl=en&lr=&id=9HE-DQAAQBAJ&oi=fnd&pg=PP1&dq=Hofstede,+2001&ots=lMv8sRy2SV&sig=ily-H197XfSVeSprBuqDUidd9gU

Hommerich, C., & Tiefenbach, T. (2018). Analyzing the Relationship between Social Capital and Subjective Well-Being: The Mediating Role of Social Affiliation. *Journal of Happiness Studies, 19*, 1091–1114.

Infant Mortality. (2024). *2024*. https://bala.stat.gov.kz/en/mladencheskaya-smertnost/

Inglehart, R. (1997). Modernization, Postmodernization and Changing Perceptions of Risk. *International Review of Sociology, 7*(3), 449–459. https://doi.org/10.1080/03906701.1997.9971250

Inglehart, R. (2020). *Modernization and Postmodernization: Cultural, Economic, and Political Change in 43 Societies*. Princeton University Press. https://books.google.com/books?hl=en&lr=&id=D9PgDwAAQBAJ&oi=fnd&pg=PA3&dq=Modernization+and+Postmodernization:+Cultural,+Economic,+and+Political+Change+in+43+Societies&ots=OKDoIRQler&sig=LLBf1E6othLO23tVttaQMIilfCU

Inglehart, R., C. Haerpfer, A. Moreno, C. Welzel, K. Kizilova, J. Diez-Medrano, M. Lagos, P. Norris, E. Ponarin & B. Puranen et al. (eds.). (2018a). *World Values Survey: Round Six - Country Pooled Datafile*. Madrid, Spain & Vienna, Austria: JD Systems Institute & WVSA Secretariat. https://doi.org/10.14281/18241.8

Inglehart, R., C. Haerpfer, A. Moreno, C. Welzel, K. Kizilova, J. Diez-Medrano, M. Lagos, P. Norris, E. Ponarin & B. Puranen et al. (eds.). (2018b). *World Values Survey: Round Four - Country Pooled Datafile*. Madrid, Spain & Vienna, Austria: JD Systems Institute & WVSA Secretariat. https://doi.org/10.14281/18241.6

Inoguchi, T., & Fujii, S. (2012). *The Quality of Life in Asia: A Comparison of Quality of Life in Asia*. Springer Science & Business Media.

Kalmijn, M. (2005). The Effects of Divorce on Men's Employment and Social Security Histories. *European Journal of Population / Revue Européenne De Démographie, 21*(4), 347–366. https://doi.org/10.1007/s10680-005-0200-7

Kalyuzhnova, Y., & Patterson, K. (2016). Kazakhstan: Long-Term Economic Growth and the Role of the Oil Sector. *Comparative Economic Studies, 58*(1), 93–118. https://doi.org/10.1057/ces.2015.31

Kamp, M. (2009). Women's Studies and Gender Studies in Central Asia: Are We Talking to One Another. *Central Eurasian Studies Review, 8*(1), 2–12.

Kamp, M., & Nurdinova, S. (2022). Uzbek Migrants in Türkiye. *The Region, 11*(2), 193–210.

Kim, S. (2023). Comparison of Happiness Levels in Central Asian Countries. *Journal of the Korea Society of Computer and Information, 28*(6), 145–152.

Kudebayeva, A., Sharipova, A., & Sharipova, D. (2022). Social Capital and Subjective Well-Being in Central Asia. *Europe-Asia Studies, 74*(1), 101–124. https://doi.org/10.1080/09668136.2021.1973965

Kuroki, M. (2011). Does Social Trust Increase Individual Happiness in JAPAN?*: M. Kuroki: Happiness and Trust. *Japanese Economic Review, 62*(4), 444–459. https://doi.org/10.1111/j.1468-5876.2011.00533.x

Laruelle, M., Huchet, J. F., Peyrouse, S., & Balci, B. (2010). Why Central Asia? The Strategic Rationale of Indian and Chinese Involvement in the Region. In Laruelle, M., Huchet, J. –F., Peyrouse, S., & Balci, B. (Eds.), *China and India in Central Asia* (pp. 1–6). Palgrave Macmillan US. https://doi.org/10.1057/9780230114357_1

Li, J., Chen, Y., Li, Z., & Huang, X. (2019). Low-Carbon Economic Development in Central Asia Based on LMDI Decomposition and Comparative Decoupling Analyses. *Journal of Arid Land, 11*(4), 513–524. https://doi.org/10.1007/s40333-019-0063-0

Life Expectancy at Birth of the Population of the Republic of Kazakhstan. (2023). *2023*. https://stat.gov.kz/en/industries/social-statistics/demography/publications/157663/

Lu, H., Tong, P., & Zhu, R. (2020). Longitudinal Evidence on Social Trust and Happiness in China: Causal Effects and Mechanisms. *Journal of Happiness Studies, 21*, 1841–1858.

Luhmann, M., Hofmann, W., Eid, M., & Lucas, R. E. (2012). Subjective Well-Being and Adaptation to Life Events: A Meta-Analysis. *Journal of Personality and Social Psychology, 102*(3), 592.

Makulbayeva, G. A., Davletbayeva, Zh. Zh., & Dyussenov, M. M. (2023). *Subjective Well-Being in Central Asia: Rural-Urban Differences, 145*(4), 363–373.

Marat, E. (2006). *The Tulip Revolution: Kyrgyzstan One Year After*. Jamestown Foundation. https://www.academia.edu/download/12961445/The_Tulip_Revolution.pdf

Marmot, M., & Bobak, M. (2005). Social and Economic Changes and Health in Europe East and West. *European Review, 13*(1), 15–31.

Matsushima, M., & Matsunaga, Y. (2015). Social Capital and Subjective Well-Being in Japan. *VOLUNTAS: International Journal of Voluntary and Nonprofit Organizations*, 26, 1016–1045.

McKee-Ryan, F., Song, Z., Wanberg, C. R., & Kinicki, A. J. (2005). Psychological and Physical Well-Being During Unemployment: A Meta-Analytic Study. *Journal of Applied Psychology, 90*(1), 53.

Meeks, R. (2012). *Culture and Gender Roles: Evidence from a Natural Experiment in Post-Soviet Central Asia*. https://www.dartmouth.edu/neudc2012/docs/paper_258.pdf

Megoran, N. (2010). The Uzbekistan-Kyrgyzstan Boundary: Stalin's Cartography, Post-Soviet Geography. *Borderliness and Borderlands: Political Oddities at the Edge of the Nation-State*, 33–52.

Migration and Development Brief 38 | KNOMAD. (2023). *2023*. https://knomad.org/publication/migration-and-development-brief-38

Myers, D. G. (2000). The Funds, Friends, and Faith of Happy People. *American Psychologist, 55*(1), 56.

Naghdi, Y., Amirtaemeh, H., & Kaghazian, S. (2021). The Puzzle of Relationship between the Economic Growth and Happiness. *Economic Analysis, 54*(1), 1–12.

Nations United. (2024). *Human Development Report 2023–24. Human Development Reports*. United Nations. https://hdr.undp.org/content/human-development-report-2023-24

Neira Gómez, I., Lacalle-Calderón, M., Portela, M., & Pérez Trujillo, M. (n.d.). *Social Capital Dimensions and Subjective Wellbeing: A Quantile Approach*. Accessed April 16, 2024. https://minerva.usc.es/xmlui/handle/10347/32144

Omarova, A., & Kenzhakimov, G. (2023). Sociological Measurement of the Happiness Index in Central Asian Countries. *Journal of Community Positive Practices, 1*, 17–28.

Oreopoulos, P. (2008). Priceless: The Nonpecuniary Benefits of Schooling. *Journal of Economic Perspectives, 25*(1), 1516.

Osmonova, D., Talgarbekova, E., Tashtanbekova, M., Moldoshova, A., & Anastassiadi, A. (2023). Evolution of Family Relationship in Kyrgyzstan. *Social and Legal Studios, 6*(4), 155–163.

Population: Official Statistics—Statistics of the Kyrgyz Republic. (2024). *2024*. https://stat.gov.kg/en/statistics/naselenie/

Population of the Republic of Kazakhstan by Gender and Type of Locality. (2024, April 1). *2024*. https://stat.gov.kz/en/industries/social-statistics/demography/publications/159623/

Portela, M., Neira, I., & Salinas-Jiménez, M. D. M. (2013). Social Capital and Subjective Wellbeing in Europe: A New Approach on Social Capital. *Social Indicators Research,* 114(2), 493–511. https://doi.org/10.1007/s11205-012-0158-x

Puntscher, S., Hauser, C., Walde, J., & Tappeiner, G. (2015). The Impact of Social Capital on Subjective Well-Being: A Regional Perspective. *Journal of Happiness Studies, 16*, 1231–1246.

Ram, R. (2010). Social Capital and Happiness: Additional Cross-Country Evidence. *Journal of Happiness Studies, 11*(4), 409–418. https://doi.org/10.1007/s10902-009-9148-3

Rosenfeld, M. J., & Roesler, K. (2019). Stability and Change in Predictors of Marital Dissolution in the US 1950–2015: The Rise of Family Inequality. In *Presented at the American Sociological Association Meetings in New York. [Google Scholar]*. http://web.stanford.edu/~mrosenfe/Rosenfeld_and_Roesler_divorce_inequality.pdf

Ryff, C. D., & Boylan, J. M. (2016). Linking Happiness to Health: Comparisons between Hedonic and Eudaimonic Well-Being. *Handbook of Research Methods and Applications in Happiness and Quality of Life*, 53–70.

Selim, S. (2008). Life Satisfaction and Happiness in Turkey. *Social Indicators Research, 88*, 531–562.

Sen, A. (2006). Reason, Freedom and Well-Being. *Utilitas, 18*(1), 80–96.

Serikbayeva, B., & Abdulla, K. (2022). Good Governance Matters for Well-Being: The Case of Kazakhstan. *Transforming Government: People, Process and Policy, 16*(1), 140–164.

Sharipova, D., & Kudebayeva, A. (2023a). Changing Well-Being in Central Asia: Evidence from Kazakhstan and Kyrgyzstan. *Journal of Happiness Studies, 24*(3), 1233–1260.

Sharipova, D., & Kudebayeva, A. (2023b). Changing Well-Being in Central Asia: Evidence from Kazakhstan and Kyrgyzstan. *Journal of Happiness Studies, 24*(3), 1233–1260. https://doi.org/10.1007/s10902-022-00607-1

Spechler, M. C. (2008). The Economies of Central Asia: A Survey. *Comparative Economic Studies, 50*(1), 30–52. https://doi.org/10.1057/ces.2008.3

Suh, E., Diener, Ed., & Fujita, F. (1996). Events and Subjective Well-Being: Only Recent Events Matter. *Journal of Personality and Social Psychology,* 70(5), 1091.

Temirkulov, A. (2010). Kyrgyz 'Revolutions' in 2005 and 2010: Comparative Analysis of Mass Mobilization. *Nationalities Papers, 38*(5), 589–600.

Timur, D. (2006). Living Conditions, Intra-Societal Trust, and Public Concerns in Post-Socialist Turkmenistan. *Central Asia and the Caucasus, 4*(40), 122–132.

Tokhirov, A. (2023). *Income Fluctuations and Subjective Well-Being: Partially Mediating Effects of Remittances.* IOS Working Papers. https://www.econstor.eu/handle/10419/273577

Umberson, D., Williams, K., Powers, D. A., Chen, M. D., & Campbell, A. M. (2005). As Good as It Gets? A Life Course Perspective on Marital Quality. *Social Forces, 84*(1), 493–511.

Uzbekistan Pilot Multidimensional Poverty Index Report 2023: Poverty and Deprivation Analysis Using the Multidimensional Poverty Index (MPI) | OPHI. (2023). *2023.* https://ophi.org.uk/publications/Uzbekistan-MPI-2023

Veenhoven, R. (1984). The Concept of Happiness. In R. Veenhoven (Ed.), *Conditions of Happiness* (pp. 12–38). Springer Netherlands. https://doi.org/10.1007/978-94-009-6432-7_2

Veenhoven, R. (2016). Quality of Life and Happiness: Concepts and Measures. In *Handbook of Research Methods and Applications in Happiness and Quality of Life* (pp. 309–333). Edward Elgar Publishing. https://www.elgaronline.com/abstract/edcoll/9781783471164/9781783471164.00020.xml

Waite, L., & Gallagher, M. (2001). *The Case for Marriage: Why Married People Are Happier, Healthier and Better off Financially.* Crown.

Welzel, C., & Inglehart, R. (2001). *Human Development and the "Explosion" of Democracy: Variations of Regime Change across 60 Societies.* https://www.ssoar.info/ssoar/handle/document/11513

Wilkinson, R. G., & Pickett, K. E. (2009). Income Inequality and Social Dysfunction. *Annual Review of Sociology, 35*(1), 493–511. https://doi.org/10.1146/annurev-soc-070308-115926

Winkelmann, R. (2009). Unemployment, Social Capital, and Subjective Well-Being. *Journal of Happiness Studies, 10*, 421–430.

World Bank Open Data. (2024). https://data.worldbank.org

Yamada, E., Shimizutani, S., & Murakami, E. (2022). Remittances, Household Welfare, and the COVID-19 Pandemic in Tajikistan. *Asian Development Review, 39*(02), 147–174. https://doi.org/10.1142/S0116110522500159

Chapter 4
Happiness from a Political Perspective in Central Asia

Abstract This chapter explores the intricate relationship between political dynamics and the well-being of individuals and communities in Central Asia. The study draws upon historical, cultural, and contemporary political insights to explore the factors influencing happiness and the role of governance in shaping subjective well-being in the region. Central Asia's diverse linguistic, religious, and historical landscape has contributed to a complex political terrain, influenced by historical legacies, post-Soviet transitions, and geopolitical factors. Through an examination of the challenges faced by Central Asia, including economic disparities, governance issues, and social transformations, the study aims to offer a nuanced understanding of the political dimensions of well-being. This research also seeks to identify opportunities for positive political interventions that can enhance happiness and societal welfare for holistic development in the region. The study utilizes World Value Survey data to estimate subjective well-being in Central Asia from a political perspective.

Keywords Political dynamics · Central Asia · Governance · Subjective well-being · Post-Soviet transition · World Values Survey

4.1 Introduction

This chapter aims to explore the multifaceted relationship between political dynamics and the well-being of individuals and communities in the Central Asian context. Drawing on historical, cultural, and contemporary political insights, this chapter investigates the factors that influence happiness and the role of governance in shaping the subjective experiences of well-being in the region. Central Asia, comprising countries with diverse languages, religious groups, and distinct histories, presents a complex political terrain. The region's political dynamics have been shaped by historical legacies, post-Soviet transitions, and geopolitical influences. The interplay of governance structures, state-building processes, and ideological frameworks has significant implications for the well-being of the populace. The historical interactions and cultural exchanges in Central Asia have contributed to the formation of unique

S. Nurdinova, *Happiness and Life Satisfaction in Central Asia*, Quality of Life in Asia 24, https://doi.org/10.1007/978-981-95-3082-3_4

societal norms and value systems. Exploring the historical narratives and cultural heritage of the region provides valuable insights into the factors that have traditionally influenced the perception of happiness and well-being among Central Asian communities. The impact of political change on the well-being of individuals in Central Asia is a critical aspect of understanding happiness from a political perspective. Transitions in governance, policy reforms, and socioeconomic developments have direct and indirect effects on quality of life, social cohesion, and individual fulfillment within a region. Central Asia faces a myriad of challenges, including economic disparities, governance issues, and social transformations. Examining how these challenges intersect with the pursuit of happiness offers a nuanced understanding of the political dimensions of well-being. Additionally, identifying opportunities for positive political interventions that enhance happiness and societal welfare is essential for holistic development in the region. As indicated by Bhuiyan (2012), the relationship between political dynamics and the well-being of individuals and communities is a topic of significant interest, particularly in the context of Central Asia. This region, with its diverse languages, religious groups, and distinct histories, presents a complex political terrain that necessitates a deeper exploration of the factors shaping happiness and well-being. Governance structures, state-building processes, and ideological frameworks have significant implications for the well-being of the populace in Central Asia. Furthermore, understanding the historical narratives and cultural heritage of the region provides valuable insights into the factors that have traditionally influenced the perception of happiness and well-being among Central Asian communities. The impact of political change on the well-being of individuals in Central Asia is a critical aspect that requires understanding from a political perspective. As identified by Serikbayeva and Abdulla (2022), governance reforms, freedom of choice, and financial satisfaction have a substantial impact on the subjective well-being of individuals, shedding light on the evolving dynamics of governance and well-being in the region. In addition, the challenges faced by Central Asia, including economic disparities, governance issues, and social transformations, intersect with the pursuit of happiness and offer a nuanced understanding of the political dimensions of well-being. This suggests the need for positive political interventions that can enhance happiness and societal welfare for holistic development in the region. To estimate subjective well-being in Central Asia from a political perspective, World Value Survey data are used.

4.2 Governance and Subjective Well-Being in Kazakhstan

Kazakhstan's governance and its impact on subjective well-being have been the subject of significant research and analysis. This chapter aims to explore the intricate relationship between governance and the subjective well-being of individuals in Kazakhstan, drawing on empirical evidence and scholarly insights.

Political stability has been a central feature of Kazakhstan's governance since its independence (Bhuiyan, 2012). The country has experienced relative stability under the leadership of Nursultan Nazarbayev, who served as president from 1991 to 2019. Nazarbayev's administration was characterized by a focus on maintaining stability and fostering economic growth, which has both positive and negative implications for governance.

Kazakhstan has implemented substantial economic and public administration reforms since its independence in 1991. These reforms have provided an interesting case study for exploring how people perceive the outcomes of governance reforms and their impact on subjective well-being. The relationship between life satisfaction and governance reforms has been a subject of estimation and analysis, shedding light on the evolving dynamics of governance and well-being in the country (Serikbayeva & Abdulla, 2022). Sharipova and Kudebayeva (2023) identify freedom of choice and financial satisfaction as powerful factors predicting changes in subjective well-being, shedding light on the dynamics of well-being in Kazakhstan (Table 4.1).

The mean happiness score in Wave 6 is 3.20, with a standard deviation of 0.63, whereas in Wave 7, the mean happiness score is 3.22, with a standard deviation of 0.61. Similarly, the mean life satisfaction score in Wave 6 was 7.25, with a standard deviation of 2.10, and in Wave 7, the mean life satisfaction score was 7.05, with a standard deviation of 2.11. The mean score for government responsibility in Wave 6 was 4.02, with a standard deviation of 2.95, and in Wave 7, the mean score was 4.89, with a standard deviation of 2.81. The political scale has a mean of 6.18 and a standard deviation of 2.17. The confidence in government has a mean of 2.51 with a standard deviation of 0.83 in Wave 6, and in Wave 7, the mean is 2.08 with a standard deviation of 0.80. The mean age in Wave 6 was 40.02 years, with a standard deviation of 15.35, and in Wave 7, the mean age was 41.86 years, with a standard deviation of 13.93.

In Wave 6, approximately 19.8% of the individuals were categorized as single, 82.6% as married, and 17.4% as divorced. In Wave 7, the percentages changed to approximately 13.5% for single individuals, 67.3% for married individuals, and 19.1% for divorced individuals (Table 4.2).

The data show that approximately 39.6% of the respondents in Wave 6 were male, whereas approximately 44.9% were male in Wave 7. The percentage of employed individuals increased from approximately 63.9% in Wave 6 to approximately 67.7% in Wave 7. The percentage of unemployed individuals decreased from approximately 6.4% in Wave 6 to approximately 5.1% in Wave 7. The percentage of individuals out of the labor force decreased from approximately 29.7% in Wave 6 to approximately 27.2% in Wave 7. The mean income scale in Wave 6 was 5.297333, with a standard deviation of 1.95, whereas in Wave 7, the mean increased to 5.62, with a standard deviation of 1.63. This indicates a slight increase in the average income scale from Wave 6 to Wave 7, with a decrease in the variability of income levels.

In Wave 6, the mean number of children was 1.64, with a standard deviation of 1.42, and in Wave 7, the mean increased to 1.87, with a standard deviation of 1.41. This suggests a slight increase in the average number of children, with a relatively consistent level of variability in the number of children across both waves.

The mean state of health in Wave 6 was 2.31, with a standard deviation of 0.77, and in Wave 7, the mean decreased to 2.20, with a standard deviation of 0.74. This

Table 4.1 Variable definitions

Variable	Definition
Life satisfaction	All things considered, how satisfied are you with your life as a whole these days? (1) completely dissatisfied to (10) completely satisfied
Happiness	Taking all things together, would you say you are (1) not at all happy, (2) not very happy, (3) rather happy, (4) very happy?
Government's responsibility	(1) The government should take more responsibility to (10) the government should not take responsibility
Political scale	Self-positioning in the political scale: (1) left to (10) right
Confidence: government	Confidence in the government: (1) a great deal to (4) not at all
Political system	To what extent are the opinions of people like you taken into account by the political system when making important government decisions? (1) a great deal to (4) not at all
Vote in national elections	Voting in national elections: (1) always to (4) not at all
Democratic system	Governments tax the rich and subsidize the poor: (1) not an essential characteristic of democracy to (10) essential characteristic of democracy
Importance of politics	Importance of politics in life: (1) very important to (4) not at all important
Age	Your age in years
Gender	(0) typically represents female respondents; (1) typically represents male respondents
Marital status	Marital status is represented as dummy variables, where each category (married, single, divorced) is coded as (1) or (0)
Employment status	Employment status is represented as dummy variables: (1) employed (full-time, part-time, self-employed), (0) unemployed (actively seeking employment), and (0) out of the labor market (retired, homemaker, student)
Income scale	Income scale where (1) indicates the lowest income group and (10) indicates the highest income group in your country
Health status	State of health (subjective): (1) very good to (5) very poor
Financial satisfaction	Satisfaction with the financial situation of the household: (1) completely dissatisfied to (10) completely satisfied
Number of children	How many children do you have?

indicates a slight decrease in the average state of health from Wave 6 to Wave 7, with a relatively consistent level of variability in the reported state of health.

In Wave 6, the mean financial satisfaction score was 6.05, with a standard deviation of 2.44, and in Wave 7, the mean score increased to 6.37, with a standard deviation of 2.07. This suggests a slight increase in average financial satisfaction from Wave 6 to Wave 7, with a decrease in the variability of reported financial satisfaction levels.

The table shows the regression results for happiness and life satisfaction. For life satisfaction, an increase in the perception of government or individual responsibility

Table 4.2 Descriptive statistics

Variable	Wave 6 Mean	Wave 6 Std. Dev	Wave 7 Mean	Wave 7 Std. Dev	Min	Max
Happiness	3.20	0.63	3.22	0.61	1	4
Life satisfaction	7.25	2.10	7.05	2.11	1	10
Government responsibility	4.02	2.95	4.89	2.81	1	10
Political scale	6.18	2.17	–	–	1	10
Confidence: government	2.51	0.83	2.08	0.80	1	4
Political system	–	–	2.56	1.02	1	5
Vote in national election	1.63	0.72	1.74	0.73	1	3
Democratic system	6.84	2.10	6.61	2.10	1	10
Important: politics	2.59	0.87	2.55	0.93	1	4
Age	40.02	15.35	41.86	13.93	18	88
Single	0.20	0.40	0.14	0.34	0	1
Married	0.83	0.38	0.67	0.47	0	1
Divorced	0.17	0.38	0.19	0.39	0	1
Gender	0.40	0.49	0.45	0.50	0	1
Income scale	5.30	1.95	5.62	1.63	1	10
Number of children	1.64	1.42	1.87	1.41	0	8
State of health	2.31	0.77	2.20	0.74	1	4
Financial satisfaction	6.05	2.44	6.37	2.07	1	10
Employed	0.64	0.48	0.68	0.47	0	1
Unemployed	0.06	0.24	0.05	0.22	0	1
Out of labor market	0.30	0.46	0.27	0.45	0	1
N	1500	–	857	–	–	–

is associated with a slight increase in life satisfaction ($\beta = 0.05$), suggesting that individuals who perceive a lower level of government responsibility tend to report somewhat higher life satisfaction. A higher political scale score, indicating a more extreme position on the political spectrum, is negatively associated with life satisfaction ($\beta = -0.05$). This suggests that individuals who align more with the right scale tend to experience lower life satisfaction. There is no significant effect on happiness.

Confidence in the government has a negative effect on happiness (β = −0.17), meaning that lower confidence in the government is associated with decreased happiness. Confidence in government negatively affects life satisfaction. In Wave 7, the coefficient for confidence in government is β = −0.17, with a p value indicating significance at the 0.05 level. This significant negative coefficient indicates that lower confidence in the government is associated with lower life satisfaction. This means that in Wave 7, individuals with less confidence in their government reported lower levels of life satisfaction. The coefficient for confidence in government is β = −0.08, with a p value indicating significance at the 0.01 level. This significant negative effect implies that lower confidence in the government is also associated with lower happiness. Therefore, in Wave 7, a decrease in confidence in the government led to a reduction in happiness.

Support for governments taxes the rich and subsidizes the poor, as the democratic system has a significant positive effect on life satisfaction (β = 0.10), indicating that a stronger belief in the democratic system is related to greater life satisfaction.

Valuing politics highly is associated with a decrease in happiness (β = −0.07), suggesting that those who place greater importance on politics tend to have lower levels of happiness.

Age is associated with a minor decrease in happiness, suggesting that as people age, their happiness may slightly decline, although the effect is relatively small.

A higher income scale is positively associated with life satisfaction (β = 0.18), indicating that greater income is related to higher life satisfaction. The number of children has a significant positive effect on both life satisfaction (β = 0.17) and happiness (β = 0.07), suggesting that having more children is associated with increased levels of both life satisfaction and happiness. This finding aligns with research suggesting that children can provide emotional fulfillment and a sense of purpose (Luhmann et al., 2012).

A poor state of health is significantly negatively associated with both life satisfaction (β = −0.66) and happiness (β = −0.25), indicating that individuals in poorer health report lower levels of both life satisfaction and happiness.

Financial satisfaction is significantly negatively associated with life satisfaction (β = −0.10) and, to a lesser extent, with happiness (β = −0.03) in Wave 6. This finding contradicts the literature. Financial satisfaction also has a significant positive effect on both life satisfaction and happiness, underscoring its importance for well-being (Diener & Biswas-Diener, 2002).

Employment status has notable effects, with being employed negatively impacting life satisfaction (β = −0.26) in Wave 6, indicating that employed individuals might experience lower life satisfaction than those outside the labor force. Unemployment is associated with a significant decrease in life satisfaction (β = −0.59). Unemployment is associated with a significant decrease in life satisfaction, supporting the view that job loss has severe negative consequences for well-being (McKee-Ryan et al., 2005).

In Wave 7, government responsibility did not significantly impact either life satisfaction or happiness, in contrast with its effect in Wave 6.

Confidence in government negatively affects life satisfaction ($\beta = -0.17$) and happiness ($\beta = -0.08$), demonstrating that a lack of confidence in the government leads to lower levels of both life satisfaction and happiness.

Voting in national elections is negatively associated with life satisfaction ($\beta = -0.17$) in Wave 7, suggesting that the act of voting might be linked to lower life satisfaction, although it does not significantly affect happiness.

A poor state of health is significantly negatively associated with both life satisfaction ($\beta = -0.38$) and happiness ($\beta = -0.25$), indicating that poor health significantly decreases both life satisfaction and happiness. Financial satisfaction is positively associated with life satisfaction ($\beta = 0.52$) and happiness ($\beta = 0.04$), suggesting that greater financial satisfaction leads to higher levels of both life satisfaction and happiness (Table 4.3).

This analysis of survey data from Waves 6 and 7 reveals key insights into the factors affecting life satisfaction and happiness among respondents, with significant variations and trends observed between the waves. The results emphasize the complex interplay between individual perceptions, socioeconomic factors, and political attitudes. In summary, this analysis highlights the multifaceted nature of life satisfaction and happiness, which are influenced by a combination of socioeconomic, political, and personal factors. While some trends remain consistent with the literature, such as the positive impact of financial satisfaction and the negative effects of poor health, the variations between waves suggest dynamic changes in the factors influencing well-being. Future research could further explore these shifts and their underlying causes to provide deeper insights into the determinants of life satisfaction and happiness.

4.3 Revolution, Political Situation, and Happiness in Kyrgyzstan

Kyrgyzstan, a Central Asian country with a history of political upheaval, offers a compelling case for examining how revolutions and political instability impact individual happiness. Since gaining independence from the Soviet Union in 1991, Kyrgyzstan has experienced two major revolutions—one in 2005 and another in 2010—each significantly altering its political landscape. This chapter explores how these revolutionary events and the ensuing political conditions have influenced the happiness and well-being of Kyrgyz citizens. By analyzing the relationships among political instability, governance, and subjective well-being, this chapter aims to provide insights into the broader implications of political upheaval for individual happiness.

Kyrgyzstan's post-Soviet political history is characterized by periods of significant instability and change. The country has witnessed two major revolutions:

1. The Tulip Revolution (2005): This revolution led to the ousting of President Askar Akayev, who had been accused of corruption and authoritarianism. The

Table 4.3 Political factors and subjective well-being in Kazakhstan

Variable	Wave 6 life satisfaction	Wave 6 happiness	Wave 7 life satisfaction	Wave 7 happiness
Government responsibility	0.05*	0.00	−0.00	0.01
Political scale	−0.05*	−0.00		
Confidence: government	−0.06	0.02	−0.17*	−0.08**
Vote in national election	−0.11	−0.03	−0.17*	0.01
Democratic system	0.10***	0.01	0.05	0.02
Political system			0.10	−0.01
Important: politics	−0.08	−0.07***	0.00	−0.00
Age	−0.00	−0.00*	−0.00	0.00
Single	0.08	0.04	(Omitted)	(Omitted)
Married	(Omitted)	(Omitted)	0.15	−0.01
Divorced	−0.43**	−0.16***	0.19	−0.01
Gender	−0.15	−0.06	−0.15	−0.05
Income scale	0.18***	0.01	0.05	0.00
Number of children	0.17***	0.07***	0.08	0.03
State of health	−0.66***	−0.25***	−0.38***	−0.25***
Financial satisfaction	−0.10***	−0.03***	0.52***	0.04**
Employed	−0.26*	−0.16***	0.03	−0.04
Unemployed	−0.59**	−0.11	(Omitted)	(Omitted)
Out of labor market	(Omitted)	(Omitted)	−0.32	−0.09

Legend *$p < 0.05$; **$p < 0.01$; ***$p < 0.001$

revolution was characterized by widespread protests and a popular movement advocating for democratic reforms (Cummings & Ryabkov, 2013; Marat, 2006).

2. The Kyrgyz Revolution (2010): The second revolution resulted in the removal of President Kurmanbek Bakiyev, who faced allegations of corruption and authoritarian rule. The 2010 revolution led to significant political reorganization and a shift toward a more parliamentary system (Gullette, 2010; Temirkulov, 2010).

These revolutionary events have had profound effects on Kyrgyzstan's political landscape, including changes in governance, political institutions, and civil liberties. The transitional nature of the political environment has created both opportunities and challenges for the country's development (Table 4.4).

Table 4.4 Variable definitions

Variable	Definition
Life satisfaction	All things considered, how satisfied are you with your life as a whole these days? (1 = completely dissatisfied to 10 = completely satisfied)
Happiness	Taking all things together, would you say you are (1 = not at all happy, 2 = not very happy, 3 = rather happy, 4 = very happy)
Democracy	How democratically is this country being governed today? (1 = not at all democratic to 10 = very democratic)
Importance of democracy	Importance of democracy (1 = not at all important to 10 = very important)
Vote in elections	Vote in elections at the national level: (1 = always, 4 = not at all)
Satisfaction with democracy	Satisfaction with the way democracy develops (1 = very satisfied to 4 = not at all satisfied)
Political system	Assessment of the political system: (1 = very good to 4 = very bad)
Political scale	Self-positioning on the left–right political scale (1 = left to 10 = right)
Interest in politics	Interest in politics (1 = very interested to 4 = not at all interested)
Importance of politics	Indicate how important politics are in your life (1 = very important to 4 = not at all important)
Gender	0 typically represents female respondents; 1 typically represents male respondents
Age	Your age in years
Educational level	Highest educational level attained: Respondent's education ranges from early childhood education (0) to the highest level
Marital status	Marital status is represented as dummy variables, where each category (married, single, divorced) is coded as 1 or 0
Financial satisfaction	Satisfaction with the financial situation of the household (1 = completely dissatisfied to 10 = completely satisfied)

Happiness has increased from Wave 4 to Wave 6, with the mean rising from 3.07 to 3.32. The standard deviation has decreased slightly, suggesting a more concentrated distribution of happiness scores around the mean in Wave 6. The mean score for democracy level is 5.99, suggesting a moderately positive view of democracy among respondents. The standard deviation indicates some variability in responses, but the range shows that opinions on democracy span the full scale from 1 to 10. The mean score for the importance of democracy is 7.89, indicating that respondents place high importance on democracy. The mean for voting in elections is 1.37, with responses ranging from 1 to 3. The mean satisfaction with democracy is 2.83, suggesting a generally low level of satisfaction. The mean for views on the political system is 1.97, which is relatively low. The mean score for the political scale has increased to right party from Wave 4 to Wave 6, suggesting a shift in attitudes or perceptions related to politics (Table 4.5).

Interest in politics decreased from Wave 4 to Wave 6. The mean score decreases from 2.53 to 2.22, indicating reduced political interest. The standard deviation is relatively stable, suggesting consistent variability in political interest. The importance of politics slightly decreased from Wave 4 to Wave 6. The mean score decreased from 2.50 to 2.42, reflecting a slight decline. The gender distribution is fairly balanced in both waves, with a slight increase in the proportion of male respondents from Wave 4 to Wave 6. The average age of the respondents increased from 36.51 in Wave 4 to 38.73 in Wave 6. The mean educational level slightly increased from Wave 4 to Wave 6. In Wave 6, approximately 76.1% of the respondents were married. The standard

Table 4.5 Descriptive statistics

Variable	Wave 6 Mean	Wave 6 Std. Dev	Wave 4 Mean	Wave 4 Std. Dev	Min	Max
Happiness	3.32	0.55	3.07	0.59	1	4
Life satisfaction	6.94	2.16	6.64	2.48	1	10
Democracy	5.99	2.45	–	–	1	10
Importance of democracy	7.89	2.20	–	–	1	10
Vote election	1.37	0.55	–	–	1	3
Satisfaction with democracy	–	–	2.83	0.73	1	4
Political system	–	–	1.97	0.75	1	4
Political scale	6.54	2.33	6.20	2.39	1	10
Interest in politics	2.22	0.91	2.53	0.92	1	4
Importance politics	2.42	0.84	2.50	0.93	1	4
Gender	0.49	0.50	0.44	0.50	0	1
Age	38.73	14.37	36.51	15.03	18	89
Educational level	6.78	1.93	6.72	1.93	1	9
Married	0.76	0.43	0.62	0.49	0	1
Single	0.16	0.36	0.26	0.44	0	1
Divorced	0.08	0.28	0.13	0.34	0	1
Financial satisfaction	–	–	5.80	2.50	1	10
N	1402	–	854	–	–	–

deviation of 0.43 indicates variability around this mean, but most respondents are married. Approximately 15.5% of the respondents were single, and approximately 8.3% of the respondents were divorced. In Wave 4, approximately 62.2% of the respondents were married. This value is lower than that in Wave 6. Approximately 25.8% of the respondents were single, and approximately 13.3% of the respondents were divorced. The mean financial satisfaction score of 5.8 indicates that, on average, respondents rate their financial satisfaction slightly above the midpoint of the scale.

The significant positive coefficient indicates that placing greater importance on democracy is associated with greater life satisfaction. This suggests that valuing democracy contributes positively to life satisfaction. A significant negative coefficient indicates that dissatisfaction with the voting process is associated with lower happiness. This suggests that respondents who are unhappy with election processes report lower levels of happiness. A positive and significant coefficient suggests that higher political scale ratings (right) are associated with increased happiness and life satisfaction. The negative and significant coefficient suggests that greater interest in politics is associated with greater life satisfaction in Wave 6 (Table 4.6).

The significant negative coefficient indicates that being female (assuming 0 = female and 1 = male) is associated with lower life satisfaction. This suggests a gender disparity in life satisfaction in wave 6. The negative and significant coefficient suggests that with each additional year of age, happiness decreases slightly. This could indicate a trend where older respondents report slightly lower happiness. A significant positive coefficient indicates that being married is associated with greater happiness and life satisfaction. The significant positive coefficient suggests that being single is also associated with greater life satisfaction/happiness than being divorced.

In wave 4, the negative and significant coefficient indicates that higher education levels are associated with slightly lower happiness. This might reflect a specific contextual factor affecting educated individuals' happiness, although this result is less common in broader studies. The significant positive coefficient shows that being married is strongly associated with greater happiness. This result aligns with the common finding that marital status positively influences happiness. Higher financial satisfaction is positively associated with greater happiness and life satisfaction. Financial stability can reduce stress and increase overall well-being, contributing to greater happiness.

The negative and statistically significant coefficient indicates that a greater importance placed on politics is associated with greater life satisfaction in Wave 4. This result suggests that individuals who place high importance on political issues may have greater life satisfaction.

The analysis of happiness and life satisfaction in Kyrgyzstan across different waves of data reveals nuanced insights into how political conditions, socioeconomic factors, and personal characteristics interact to influence individual well-being. This conclusion synthesizes the findings, contextualizes them with the relevant literature, and discusses their implications.

In Wave 6, the importance placed on democracy positively correlates with life satisfaction, supporting the notion that democratic values contribute to well-being

Table 4.6 Political factors and subjective well-being

Variable	Happiness (Wave 6)	Life satisfaction (Wave 6)	Life satisfaction (Wave 4)	Happiness (Wave 4)
Democracy	0.01	−0.02		
Importance of democracy	−0.01	0.17***		
Satisfaction with democracy		−0.08	−0.00	
Political system		−0.12	0.01	
Vote election	−0.06*	−0.16		
Political scale	0.02***	0.07*	0.04	−0.00
Interest in politics	−0.01	−0.15*	0.13	0.00
Importance politics	−0.02	−0.03	−0.19**	−0.03
Gender	−0.01	−0.23*	−0.02	0.01
Age	−0.00**	0.00	−0.01	−0.00
Education	−0.01	0.05	−0.02	−0.03**
Married	0.21***	0.63**	0.43	0.32*
Single	0.15*	0.89**	0.26	0.29
Divorced	(Omitted)	(Omitted)	(Omitted)	(Omitted)
Financial satisfaction			0.61***	0.06
_Cons	3.35***	4.96***	3.67***	2.82***
N	1402	1402	854	854
R^2	0.04	0.07	0.44	0.11

Legend $^*p < 0.05$; $^{**}p < 0.01$; $^{***}p < 0.001$

(Dolan & Peasgood, 2008). This aligns with the capability approach, which emphasizes that effective democratic governance enhances individuals' opportunities and well-being (Sen, 2006).

4.4 Political Freedom and Happiness in Tajikistan

Tajikistan, a Central Asian country with a history marked by political turmoil and socioeconomic challenges, presents a unique case for examining the relationship between political freedom and happiness. This chapter investigates how the degree of political freedom influences individual well-being in Tajikistan, exploring the complex interplay between governance, political liberties, and subjective well-being. By analyzing empirical data and contextual factors, this chapter aims to provide a comprehensive understanding of how political conditions impact happiness in this post-Soviet state.

Political freedom in Tajikistan is characterized by significant restrictions. Since its independence from the Soviet Union in 1991, Tajikistan has experienced limited democratic development, with power concentrated in the hands of the ruling elite. The country has faced issues such as restricted press freedom, limited political pluralism, and significant constraints on civil society. The ruling regime, led by President Emomali Rahmon in 1992, has maintained a tight grip on political power, leading to limited political freedoms and human rights challenges (Table 4.7).

This table explores various sociodemographic and attitudinal variables. The average reported happiness level among respondents was 3.56, with individual responses varying by approximately 0.61 units on a scale from 1 to 4. Life satisfaction, with a mean of 7.93 and a standard deviation of 1.85, indicates a spread of responses across the scale from 1 to 10. The respondents displayed moderate interest in politics (mean = 2.49 on a scale of 1–4) and considered democracy highly important (mean = 8.39 on a scale of 2–10). The respondents reported a mean score of 1.45 for the frequency of voting in national elections, with responses scattered by approximately 0.74 units. Satisfaction with politics averaged 8.08, with responses

Table 4.7 Variable definitions

Variable	Definition
Life satisfaction	Measures overall satisfaction with life, rated from 1 (completely dissatisfied) to 10 (completely satisfied)
Happiness	Assesses general happiness, where 1 is not at all happy and 4 is very happy
Interest in politics	Indicates level of interest in politics, with 1 (very interested) to 4 (not at all interested)
Importance of democracy	Rates the perceived importance of democracy from 1 (very important) to 10 (not at all important)
Vote in national elections	Reflects voting frequency in national elections, where 1 (always) to 4 (not at all)
Satisfaction with politics	Evaluates satisfaction with political system performance, rated from 1 (completely dissatisfied) to 10 (completely satisfied)
Political scale	Self-positioning on a left–right political scale, where 1 is left and 10 is right
Freedom of choice	Measures perceived freedom of choice and control, rated from 1 (no choice at all) to 10 (the highest freedom)
Gender	Coded as 0 for female respondents and 1 for male respondents
Health status	Subjective health assessment, where 1 (very good) to 5 (very poor)
Income scale	Indicates household income level, with 1 (lowest income group) to 10 (highest income group)
Marital status	Represented as dummy variables: single (0/1), married (0/1), divorced (0/1)
Employment status	Coded as dummy variables: unemployed (0/1) for those actively seeking work, employed (0/1) for full-time, part-time, or self-employed individuals, and out of labor (0/1) for retirees, homemakers, or students

varying by approximately 1.81 units on a scale from 2 to 10. The political scale mean was 7.54, indicating relatively high self-placement on a scale from 1 to 10, with a standard deviation of 2.25. The average score for perceived freedom of choice was 7.46 on a scale of 1–10, suggesting a generally favorable perception of personal freedom among respondents. Approximately half of the respondents identified as male (mean = 0.49), highlighting a balanced gender representation in the sample. Health status was moderate, with a mean of 2.09 on a scale of 1–5, indicating a mix of perceived health conditions among respondents. The respondents reported an average income satisfaction score of 5.55, with a standard deviation of 1.53, reflecting variability in perceived income levels. The vast majority of respondents were married (94.23%), with a very small percentage reporting being single (0.31%) or divorced (5.46%). Employment status varied, with 45.33% of respondents employed, 24.76% unemployed, and 29.91% out of the labor force (Table 4.8).

Variables such as the importance of democracy, voting in national elections, self-positioning on a political scale, gender and employment status did not significantly impact life satisfaction (β = -or happiness). Satisfaction with political performance had a strong positive association with life satisfaction (β = 0.17), indicating that those who are more satisfied with the political situation tend to report higher levels of life satisfaction. Perceived freedom of choice showed a significant positive relationship with life satisfaction (β = 0.30). This suggests that individuals who feel that they

Table 4.8 Descriptive statistics

Variable	Mean	Std. Dev	Min	Max
Happiness	3.56	0.61	1	4
Life satisfaction	7.93	1.85	1	10
Interest in politics	2.49	0.93	1	4
Importance of democracy	8.39	1.69	2	10
Vote in national elections	1.45	0.74	1	4
Satisfaction with politics	8.08	1.81	2	10
Political scale	7.54	2.25	1	10
Freedom of choice	7.46	2.13	1	10
Gender	0.49	0.50	0	1
Health status	2.09	0.83	1	5
Income scale	5.55	1.53	1	10
Single	0.00	0.06	0	1
Married	0.94	0.23	0	1
Divorced	0.05	0.23	0	1
Unemployed	0.25	0.43	0	1
Employed	0.45	0.50	0	1
Out of labor	0.30	0.46	0	1
N	953			

have more freedom of choice tend to report higher levels of life satisfaction and happiness. Poorer health status was negatively associated with life satisfaction ($\beta = -0.21$). Higher income satisfaction was positively associated with life satisfaction ($\beta = 0.11$), indicating that those who perceive their income more favorably tend to report higher subjective well-being. Marital status, however, was significantly correlated only with life satisfaction ($\beta = 0.77$), indicating greater life satisfaction among married individuals.

There is a statistically significant relationship between interest in politics and happiness ($\beta = -0.07$). This suggests that greater interest in politics tends to be associated with lower levels of reported happiness among respondents. Health status and happiness were negatively associated, indicating that better health was significantly related to higher happiness levels.

Higher income satisfaction was positively associated with happiness ($\beta = 0.04$). Being single or married had a significant positive relationship with happiness ($\beta = 0.36$), suggesting that individuals tend to report higher levels of happiness than their divorced counterparts do (Table 4.9).

The findings from Tajikistan are consistent with broader literature on political freedom and happiness. Studies in various contexts have demonstrated that political repression and a lack of personal freedom can negatively impact well-being

Table 4.9 Political factors and subjective well-being

Variable	Life satisfaction	Happiness
Interest in politics	−0.04	−0.07
Importance of democracy	0.08	0.02
Vote in national elections	0.05	−0.04
Satisfaction with politics	0.17***	0.02
Political scale	0.03	−0.01
Freedom of choice	0.30***	0.02
Gender	−0.04	−0.03
Health status	−0.21**	−0.19***
Income scale	0.11**	0.04**
Single	0.06	0.36**
Married	0.77**	0.23*
Divorced	(Omitted)	(Omitted)
Unemployed	(Omitted)	(Omitted)
Employed	−0.03	−0.05
Out of labor	−0.05	0.04
Constant	2.51***	3.39***
N	953	953
R^2	0.33	0.13

Legend $^{*}p < 0.05$; $^{**}p < 0.01$; $^{***}p < 0.001$

(Inglehart, 1997). The positive relationship between freedom of choice and happiness supports theories emphasizing the importance of personal agency (Alkire, 2005; Anand et al., 2005). The negative association between health status and happiness is in line with existing research highlighting the significant role of health in subjective well-being (Graham, 2008).

This chapter illustrates the significant impact of political freedom on happiness in Tajikistan. Restricted political freedoms contribute to lower levels of subjective well-being, emphasizing the need for reforms to enhance political liberties and improve overall happiness. The findings emphasize the importance of effective governance, personal agency, and socioeconomic conditions in shaping well-being. Future research should continue to explore these relationships, considering both global theories and local contexts, to provide a nuanced understanding of well-being in restrictive environments.

4.5 The New Government of Uzbekistan and Happiness

Uzbekistan, a Central Asian nation rich in history and cultural heritage, has experienced significant political and economic transformations in recent years. Since the advent of the new government under President Shavkat Mirziyoyev, Uzbekistan has been undergoing profound reforms aimed at modernizing its economy, enhancing governance, and improving the quality of life for its citizens. This chapter explores the impact of these reforms on the happiness and well-being of the Uzbek population. By examining recent data and the relevant literature, we aim to understand how political and economic changes under the new government influence the subjective well-being of Uzbeks.

Improvements in bureaucratic efficiency and a reduction in red tape can lead to a more favorable living environment. Simplified administrative procedures and reduced bureaucratic hurdles can increase individual satisfaction and ease of accessing services, contributing to overall happiness.

The new government of Uzbekistan has implemented a range of reforms that have positively impacted the happiness and well-being of its citizens. Economic modernization, improvements in governance, increased social freedom, and investments in infrastructure have contributed to higher levels of life satisfaction. However, data used for this study were collected in 2011, which did not reflect reforms on subjective well-being (Table 4.10).

On average, respondents rate their happiness at 3.70, with scores ranging from 1 (low happiness) to 4 (high happiness). The relatively low standard deviation of 0.52 indicates that happiness ratings are clustered closely around the mean. The average life satisfaction score is 7.99, with scores ranging from 1 (low satisfaction) to 10 (high satisfaction). The standard deviation of 1.76 suggests moderate variability in life satisfaction ratings among respondents.

On average, respondents perceive the existence of a democratic system at 1.37, with scores ranging from 1 to 4. The standard deviation of 0.59 indicates variability

Table 4.10 Variable definitions

Variable	Definition
Life satisfaction	A measure of overall contentment with life, rated from 1 (completely dissatisfied) to 10 (completely satisfied)
Happiness	A subjective assessment of happiness, where 1 indicates "not at all happy" and 4 indicates "very happy"
Having a democratic system	Evaluation of the political system's quality, rated from 1 (very good) to 4 (very bad)
Political influence	Perception of the influence of older individuals in politics, rated from 1 (agree strongly) to 4 (disagree strongly)
Governments tax rich	Assessment of whether taxing the rich and subsidizing the poor is essential for democracy, rated from 1 (not essential) to 10 (essential)
Government responsibility	Opinion on the extent of government responsibility, rated from 1 (should take more responsibility) to 10 (should not take responsibility)
Confidence: government	Level of confidence in the government, rated from 1 (a great deal) to 4 (not at all)
Future changes: technology	Perception of future technological changes, rated from 1 (very good) to 3 (very bad)
Future changes: work	Opinion on the decreasing importance of work in the future, rated from 1 (very good) to 3 (very bad)
Political scale	Self-positioning on a left–right political scale, where 1 represents left and 10 represents right
Importance of democracy	Assessment of the importance of democracy, rated from 1 (very important) to 10 (not at all important)
Interest in politics	Level of interest in politics, rated from 1 (very interested) to 4 (not at all interested)
Gender	Coded as 0 for female respondents and 1 for male respondents
Marital status	Represented as dummy variables for marital status categories: married, single, and divorced, coded as 1 or 0
Employment status	Coded as dummy variables: "employed" (full-time, part-time, or self-employed), "unemployed" (actively seeking employment), and "out of labor market" (retired, homemaker, or student)
Number of children	Total number of children in the household
Income scale	A scale indicating household income, where 1 represents the lowest income group and 10 represents the highest income group in the country

in perceptions about the democratic system. The average perception of political influence is 3.22, with scores ranging from 1 to 4. The standard deviation of 0.85 suggests variability in perceptions of political influence. On average, respondents rate the government's tax policies toward the rich at 6.48, with ratings ranging from 1 to 10. The standard deviation of 3.11 indicates variability in perceptions about taxation policies. The average perception of government responsibility is 4.49, with ratings ranging from 1 to 10. The standard deviation of 3.28 indicates variability in perceptions about the government's role.

On average, respondents rate their confidence in the government at 1.25, with scores ranging from 1 to 4. The average perception of future changes in technology is 1.06, with scores ranging from 1 to 3, and the standard deviation is 0.27. On average, respondents perceive future changes in work at 2.80, with scores ranging from 1 to 3. The standard deviation of 0.54 indicates variability in perceptions about future work changes.

The average political scale rating is 6.36, with ratings ranging from 1 to 10. The standard deviation of 2.07 indicates variability in the political scale. On average, respondents rate the importance of democracy at 8.87, with ratings ranging from 1 to 10. The standard deviation of 1.72 indicates variability in the importance placed on democracy. The average interest in politics is 2.33, with scores ranging from 1 to 4. The standard deviation of 0.88 indicates variability in interest levels. Gender is coded as binary (0 for female, 1 for male). The mean of 0.47 suggests that approximately 47.11% of the respondents are male, with a standard deviation of 0.50, indicating variability in the gender distribution among the respondents.

On average, respondents rate their income scale at 6.02, with ratings ranging from 1 (low income) to 10 (high income). The standard deviation of 1.61 indicates variability in income perceptions among respondents. On average, respondents have 2.53 children, with the number ranging from 0 to 8. The standard deviation of 1.82 indicates variability in the number of children among respondents.

The mean value of 0.49 indicates that approximately 49.17% of the sample is employed. This suggests a relatively balanced distribution between employed and nonemployed individuals. Approximately 12.81% of the sample is unemployed. Approximately 38.02% of the sample is out of the labor force. This percentage represents those who are neither employed nor unemployed, such as retirees, students, or those not actively seeking work.

The mean of 0.76 suggests that approximately 76.45% of the sample is married. This high proportion indicates that being married is quite common in this sample. Approximately 13.64% of the samples are single. The mean of 0.10 suggests that approximately 9.92% of the sample is divorced. This finding indicates that divorce is relatively less common than being married or single in this sample (Table 4.11).

A perception of the most favorable political influence on older people is associated with a slight increase in life satisfaction. Lower confidence in the government is strongly associated with greater life satisfaction. A higher perception on the political scale is associated with a slight increase in life satisfaction. More right-wing people have higher life satisfaction. Compared with other marital statuses, being divorced is strongly associated with lower life satisfaction. A higher income scale is strongly associated with higher life satisfaction.

The interpretation of happiness would follow a similar structure on the basis of the coefficients provided for each predictor variable. The positive and statistically significant coefficient indicates that expectations about future changes in work have a positive effect on happiness. Individuals who are pessimistic about the future of work tend to report higher happiness levels.

The positive and significant coefficient suggests that a higher political scale or a more right-wing political party is associated with increased happiness.

Table 4.11 Descriptive statistics

Variable	Mean	Std. Dev	Min	Max
Happiness	3.70	0.52	1	4
Life satisfaction	8.00	1.76	1	10
Having a democratic system	1.37	0.59	1	4
Political influence	3.22	0.85	1	4
Governments tax rich	6.48	3.11	1	10
Government responsibility	4.49	3.28	1	10
Confidence: government	1.25	0.49	1	4
Future changes: technology	1.06	0.27	1	3
Future changes: work	2.80	0.54	1	3
Political scale	6.36	2.07	1	10
Importance of democracy	8.87	1.72	1	10
Interest in politics	2.33	0.88	1	4
Gender	0.47	0.50	0	1
Employed	0.49	0.50	0	1
Unemployed	0.13	0.33	0	1
Out of labor	0.38	0.49	0	1
Married	0.76	0.42	0	1
Single	0.14	0.34	0	1
Divorced	0.10	0.30	0	1
Income scale	6.02	1.61	1	10
Number of children	2.53	1.82	0	8
N	484			

The negative and highly significant coefficient indicates that being divorced is strongly associated with lower happiness. This result highlights the substantial negative impact of divorce on individual well-being, reflecting the emotional and social challenges that often accompany divorce.

The positive and significant coefficient suggests that having more children is associated with increased happiness. A greater number of children are linked to increased happiness, suggesting the positive emotional impact of family and social support. This aligns with research indicating that children can provide significant emotional support and fulfillment (Myers, 2000). The coefficient for gender is −0.12. This negative value implies that there is a decrease in happiness associated with being female compared with the reference gender (Table 4.12).

The analysis of life satisfaction and happiness in Uzbekistan reveals several insightful patterns and relationships influenced by various sociopolitical and economic factors. Drawing from the data, key findings include the significant roles played by government confidence, political orientation, marital status, income scale, and the number of children in shaping individual well-being. These insights are

Table 4.12 Political factors and subjective well-being

Variable	Life satisfaction	Happiness
Having a democratic system	−0.17	0.03
Political influence	0.20*	−0.00
Governments tax the rich	−0.03	0.01
Government responsibility	0.03	0.00
Confidence: government	−0.68***	−0.07
Future changes: technology	−0.15	−0.23
Future changes: work	−0.04	0.09*
Political scale	0.09*	0.03
Importance of democracy	0.07	0.02
Interest in politics	−0.09	0.00
Gender	−0.11	−0.12*
Employment status		
Employed	0.08	0.08
Unemployed	−0.06	0.13
Out of labor	(Omitted)	(Omitted)
Marital status		
Married	−0.37	−0.02
Single	(Omitted)	(Omitted)
Divorced	−1.10**	−0.56***
Income scale	0.26***	0.01
Number of children	0.09	0.04*
Cons	6.46***	3.23***
N	484	484
R^2	0.22	0.17

Legend $^*p < 0.05$; $^{**}p < 0.01$; $^{***}p < 0.001$

supported by the established literature on subjective well-being and can offer valuable implications for policy and further research.

A notable finding is the strong association between confidence in the government and life satisfaction. This aligns with broader research indicating that trust in government is crucial for subjective well-being. Studies have shown that lower levels of trust in the government can lead to reduced life satisfaction and perceived quality of life (Helliwell & Putnam, 2004). These findings suggest that efforts to enhance government transparency and effectiveness could significantly improve life satisfaction among Uzbeks. Individuals with a right-leaning political stance report higher life satisfaction and happiness. This aligns with the broader theory that political stability and alignment with one's political preferences can influence well-being. Research by Welzel and Inglehart (2001) indicates that individuals who feel politically aligned with their government tend to report higher levels of satisfaction and happiness.

Individuals who are optimistic about future changes in work report higher happiness levels. This finding aligns with the positive relationship between future expectations and happiness, as optimism about future developments often correlates with greater well-being (Suh et al., 1996).

4.6 Conclusion

In conclusion, exploring the multifaceted relationship between political dynamics and subjective well-being in Central Asia sheds light on the intricate interplay between governance, culture, and societal norms.

In Uzbekistan, confidence in the government was strongly negatively associated with life satisfaction ($\beta = -0.68$, $p < 0.001$), suggesting that distrust in governance structures may significantly diminish well-being. This contrasts with some Western studies where institutional trust often correlates positively with SWB (Helliwell & Huang, 2008), highlighting potential differences in how political legitimacy is perceived in authoritarian-leaning contexts. In Tajikistan, satisfaction with politics and freedom of choice were positively linked to life satisfaction ($\beta = 0.17, p < 0.001$; $\beta = 0.30$, $p < 0.001$, respectively), aligning with Western literature emphasizing perceived autonomy as a key determinant of SWB (Inglehart et al., 2008). However, the non-significance of democratic importance in Tajikistan contrasts with Western findings, where democratic values often correlate strongly with well-being (Frey & Stutzer, 2000). Kyrgyzstan showed that the importance of democracy was positively associated with life satisfaction in Wave 6 ($\beta = 0.17, p < 0.001$), yet satisfaction with democracy was insignificant, suggesting a possible disconnect between democratic ideals and perceived governance quality. Meanwhile, Kazakhstan exhibited mixed results: while a democratic system was positively linked to life satisfaction (Wave 6: $\beta = 0.10, p < 0.001$), confidence in the government was negatively associated in Wave 7 ($\beta = -0.17, p < 0.05$), reinforcing the complexity of political trust's role in SWB.

The case of Kazakhstan offers valuable insights into the impact of governance on well-being, as evidenced by the relative stability and governance reforms implemented in the country. By further examining the intersections of governance, economic disparities, and societal transformations with the pursuit of happiness, an in-depth understanding of the political dimensions of well-being in Uzbekistan, Kyrgyzstan, and Tajikistan can be achieved. This comprehensive understanding can pave the way for identifying opportunities for positive political interventions that enhance happiness and societal welfare, thus contributing to holistic development in each of these nations. In conclusion, the exploration of governance and subjective well-being in Uzbekistan, Kyrgyzstan, and Tajikistan is essential for informed policy decisions and strategies aimed at improving the quality of life and well-being of their respective populations.

The findings emphasize the need for further research and analysis to identify opportunities for positive political interventions that can enhance happiness and societal welfare in the region. Overall, the study of governance and subjective well-being in Central Asia provides essential insights into the complex dynamics of well-being in the context of political landscapes, paving the way for informed policy decisions and holistic development in the region.

References

Abdur Rahman, A., & Veenhoven, R. (2018). Freedom and Happiness in Nations: A Research Synthesis. *Applied Research in Quality of Life, 13*(2), 435–456.

Alkire, S. (2005). Subjective Quantitative Studies of Human Agency. *Social Indicators Research, 74*(1), 217–260. https://doi.org/10.1007/s11205-005-6525-0

"Analytical tables - Agency on statistics under the President of the Republic of Tajikistan." (2023). *Агентии омори назди Президенти Ҷумҳурии Тоҷикистон* (blog). https://www.stat.tj/en/analytical-tables/

Anand, P., Hunter, G., & Smith, R. (2005). Capabilities and Well-Being: Evidence Based on the Sen-Nussbaum Approach to Welfare. *Social Indicators Research, 74*(1), 9–55. https://doi.org/10.1007/s11205-005-6518-z

Bartolini, S., Mikucka, M., & Sarracino, F. (2017). Money, Trust and Happiness in Transition Countries: Evidence from Time Series. *Social Indicators Research, 130*(1), 87–106. https://doi.org/10.1007/s11205-015-1130-3

Batsaikhan, U., & Dabrowski, M. (2017). Central Asia—Twenty-Five Years after the Breakup of the USSR. *Russian Journal of Economics, 3*(3), 296–320.

Bhuiyan, S. (2012). Political Leadership and Its Role in Achieving Good Governance in Kazakhstan. *International Journal of Public Administration, 35*(6), 379–388. https://doi.org/10.1080/01900692.2012.655525

Bian, Y., Hao, M., & Li, Y. (2018). Social Networks and Subjective Well-Being: A Comparison of Australia, Britain, and China. *Journal of Happiness Studies, 19*(8), 2489–2508. https://doi.org/10.1007/s10902-017-9926-2

Bjørnskov, C. (2003). The Happy Few: Cross-Country Evidence on Social Capital and Life Satisfaction. Available at SSRN 381640.

Bjørnskov, C. (2006). The Multiple Facets of Social Capital. *European Journal of Political Economy, 22*(1), 22–40.

Bjørnskov, C. (2008). Social Capital and Happiness in the United States. *Applied Research in Quality of Life, 3*, 43–62.

Blanchflower, D. G., & Oswald, A. J. (2008). Is Well-Being U-Shaped over the Life Cycle? *Social Science & Medicine, 66*(8), 1733–1749.

Borisova, E. (2024). *Paradoxes of Migration in Tajikistan: Locating the Good Life.* UCL Press. https://books.google.com/books?hl=en&lr=&id=S68FEQAAQBAJ&oi=fnd&pg=PP1&dq=Economic+factors+of+happiness+in+Tajikistan&ots=ptgWwZsRdp&sig=0EInHqxKn1pBlMJx71eLNZM1uZU

Brehm, J., & Rahn, W. (1997). Individual-Level Evidence for the Causes and Consequences of Social Capital. *American Journal of Political Science*, 999–1023.

Cheng, Z., & Smyth, R. (2015). Crime Victimization, Neighborhood Safety and Happiness in China. *Economic Modelling, 51*, 424–435.

Clark, A. E., Flèche, S., Layard, R., Powdthavee, N., & Ward, G. (2017). *The Key Determinants of Happiness and Misery.* https://eprints.lse.ac.uk/83622

Clark, A. E., Frijters, P., & Shields, M. A. (2006). *Income and Happiness: Evidence, Explanations and Economic Implications.* https://shs.hal.science/halshs-00590436/

Collins, K., & Gambrel, R. (2017). Corruption and Popular Support for Democracy and Government in Transitional Contexts: The Case of Kyrgyzstan. *Europe-Asia Studies, 69*(8), 1280–1309. https://doi.org/10.1080/09668136.2017.1384449

Cummings, S. N., & Ryabkov, M. (2013). Situating the 'Tulip Revolution.' In *Domestic and International Perspectives on Kyrgyzstan's 'Tulip Revolution'* (pp. 19–30). Routledge. https://doi.org/10.4324/9781315876092-4&type=chapterpdf.

Dadabaev, T. (2007). Trajectories of Political Development and Public Choices in Turkmenistan. *Asian Affairs: An American Review, 34*(3), 131–150. https://doi.org/10.3200/AAFS.34.3.131-150

Deci, E. L., & Ryan, R. M. (2012). Self-Determination Theory. *Handbook of Theories of Social Psychology, 1*(20), 416–436.

Delhey, J., Hess, S., Boehnke, K., Deutsch, F., Eichhorn, J., Kühnen, U., & Welzel, C. (2023). Life Satisfaction During the COVID-19 Pandemic: The Role of Human, Economic, Social, and Psychological Capital. *Journal of Happiness Studies, 24*(7), 2201–2222.

Demircioglu, M. A., & Sharipova, D. (2023). Does Public Sector Employment Matter for Subjective Well-Being?: The Case of Kazakhstan. *International Journal of Public Administration*, 1–16.

"Demografiya." (2024). https://stat.uz/uz/rasmiy-statistika/demography-2

Diener, A. C. (2005). Kazakhstan's Kin State Diaspora: Settlement Planning and the Oralman Dilemma. *Europe-Asia Studies, 57*(2), 327–348. https://doi.org/10.1080/09668130500052005

Diener, E. (2000). Subjective Well-Being: The Science of Happiness and a Proposal for a National Index. *American Psychologist, 55*(1), 34.

Diener, E., & Biswas-Diener, R. (2002). [No Title Found]. *Social Indicators Research, 57*(2), 119–169. https://doi.org/10.1023/A:1014411319119

Diener, E., & Chan, M. Y. (2011). Happy People Live Longer: Subjective Well-Being Contributes to Health and Longevity: HEALTH BENEFITS OF HAPPINESS. *Applied Psychology: Health and Well-Being, 3*(1), 1–43. https://doi.org/10.1111/j.1758-0854.2010.01045.x

Diener, E., Diener, C., Choi, H., & Oishi, S. (2018). Revisiting 'Most People Are Happy'—And Discovering When They Are Not. *Perspectives on Psychological Science, 13*(2), 166–170. https://doi.org/10.1177/1745691618765111.

Diener, E., & Seligman, M. E. P. (2004). Beyond Money: Toward an Economy of Well-Being. *Psychological Science in the Public Interest, 5*(1), 1–31. https://doi.org/10.1111/j.0963-7214.2004.00501001.x

Diener, E., Suh, E. M., Lucas, R. E., & Smith, H. L. (1999). Subjective Well-Being: Three Decades of Progress. *Psychological Bulletin, 125*(2), 276.

Dolan, P., & Peasgood, T. (2008). Measuring Well-Being for Public Policy: Preferences or Experiences? *The Journal of Legal Studies, 37*(S2), S5-31. https://doi.org/10.1086/595676

Easterlin, R. A. (2001). Income and Happiness: Towards a Unified Theory. *The Economic Journal, 111*(473), 465–484. https://doi.org/10.1111/1468-0297.00646

Ekici, T., & Koydemir, S. (2014). Social Capital, Government and Democracy Satisfaction, and Happiness in Turkey: A Comparison of Surveys in 1999 and 2008. *Social Indicators Research, 118*, 1031–1053.

Falkingham, J. (2000). *Women and Gender Relations in Tajikistan*. Asian Development Bank, Programs Department East and Office of Environment …. https://www.adb.org/sites/default/files/institutional-document/32601/women-tajikistan.pdf.

Flavin, P., & Keane, M. J. (2012). Life Satisfaction and Political Participation: Evidence from the United States. *Journal of Happiness Studies, 13*(1), 63–78. https://doi.org/10.1007/s10902-011-9250-1

Frey, B. S., & Stutzer, A. (2000). Happiness, economy and institutions. *The economic journal, 110*(466), 918–938.

Gauntlett, D. (2018). *Making Is Connecting: The Social Power of Creativity, from Craft and Knitting to Digital Everything*. Wiley. https://books.google.com/books?hl=en&lr=&id=VpNcDwAAQBAJ&oi=fnd&pg=PT7&dq=David+Gauntlett,+Making+Is+Connecting:+The+Social+Power+of+Creativity,+from+Craft+and+Knitting+to+Digital+Everything+(John+Wiley+%26+Sons,+2018),+&ots=3Mx4MbWysD&sig=9AfqvnDp_0FrDa5tRY9LWtUrKa8

Graham, C. (2008). Happiness And Health: Lessons—And Questions—For Public Policy. *Health Affairs, 27*(1), 72–87. https://doi.org/10.1377/hlthaff.27.1.72

Growiec, K., & Growiec, J. (2014). Trusting Only Whom You Know, Knowing Only Whom You Trust: The Joint Impact of Social Capital and Trust on Happiness in CEE Countries. *Journal of Happiness Studies, 15*(5), 1015–1040. https://doi.org/10.1007/s10902-013-9461-8

Gullette, D. (2010). Institutionalized Instability: Factors Leading to the April 2010 Uprising in Kyrgyzstan. *Eurasian Review, 3*, 89–105.

Guriev, S., & Melnikov, N. (2018). Happiness Convergence in Transition Countries. *Journal of Comparative Economics, 46*(3), 683–707.

Haerpfer, C., Inglehart, R., Moreno, A., Welzel, C., Kizilova, K., Diez-Medrano J., M. Lagos, P. Norris, E. Ponarin & B. Puranen et al. (eds.). (2020). *World Values Survey: Round Seven Country-Pooled Datafile*. Madrid, Spain & Vienna, Austria: JD Systems Institute & WVSA Secretariat. https://doi.org/10.14281/18241.1

Hagerty, M. R., & Veenhoven, R. (2003). Wealth and Happiness Revisited-Growing National Income Does Go with Greater Happiness. *Social Indicators Research, 64*, 1–27.

Harris, C. (2000). The Changing Identity of Women in Tajikistan in the Post-Soviet Period. In *Gender and Identity Construction: Women of Central Asia, the Caucasus, and Turkey, Edited by Feride Acar and Ayse G.* https://brill.com/downloadpdf/display/book/edcoll/9789004492028/B9789004492028_s013.pdf

Helliwell, J. F., & Huang, H. (2008). How's Your Government? International Evidence Linking Good Government and Well-Being. *British Journal of Political Science, 38*(4), 595–619.

Helliwell, J. F., & Putnam, R. D. (2004). The Social Context of Well–Being. In F. A. Huppert, N. Baylis, & B. Keverne (Eds.), *Philosophical Transactions of the Royal Society of London. Series B: Biological Sciences*, 359(1449), 1435–1446. https://doi.org/10.1098/rstb.2004.1522.

Hofstede, G. (2001). *Culture's Consequences: Comparing Values, Behaviors, Institutions and Organizations across Nations*. Sage Publications. https://books.google.com/books?hl=en&lr=&id=9HE-DQAAQBAJ&oi=fnd&pg=PP1&dq=Hofstede,+2001&ots=lMv8sRy2SV&sig=ily-H197XfSVeSprBuqDUidd9gU

Hommerich, C., & Tiefenbach, T. (2018). Analyzing the Relationship Between Social Capital and Subjective Well-Being: The Mediating Role of Social Affiliation. *Journal of Happiness Studies, 19*, 1091–1114.

"Infant Mortality." (2024). https://bala.stat.gov.kz/en/mladencheskaya-smertnost/

Inglehart, R. (1997). Modernization, Postmodernization and Changing Perceptions of Risk. *International Review of Sociology, 7*(3), 449–459. https://doi.org/10.1080/03906701.1997.9971250

Inglehart, R. (2020). *Modernization and Postmodernization: Cultural, Economic, and Political Change in 43 Societies*. Princeton University press. https://books.google.com/books?hl=en&lr=&id=D9PgDwAAQBAJ&oi=fnd&pg=PA3&dq=Modernization+and+Postmodernization:+Cultural,+Economic,+and+Political+Change+in+43+Societies&ots=OKDoIRQler&sig=LLBf1E6othLO23tVttaQMIilfCU

Inglehart, R., C. Haerpfer, A. Moreno, C. Welzel, K. Kizilova, J. Diez-Medrano, M. Lagos, P. Norris, E. Ponarin & B. Puranen et al. (eds.). (2018a). *World Values Survey: Round Six - Country Pooled Datafile*. Madrid, Spain & Vienna, Austria: JD Systems Institute & WVSA Secretariat. https://doi.org/10.14281/18241.8

Inglehart, R., C. Haerpfer, A. Moreno, C. Welzel, K. Kizilova, J. Diez-Medrano, M. Lagos, P. Norris, E. Ponarin & B. Puranen et al. (eds.). (2018b). *World Values Survey: Round Four - Country Pooled Datafile*. Madrid, Spain & Vienna, Austria: JD Systems Institute & WVSA Secretariat. https://doi.org/10.14281/18241.6

Inoguchi, T., & Fujii, S. (2012). *The Quality of Life in Asia: A Comparison of Quality of Life in Asia*. Springer Science & Business Media.

Kalmijn, M. (2005). The Effects of Divorce on Men's Employment and Social Security Histories. *European Journal of Population/Revue Européenne de Démographie, 21*(4), 347–366. https://doi.org/10.1007/s10680-005-0200-7

Kalyuzhnova, Y., & Patterson, K. (2016). Kazakhstan: Long-Term Economic Growth and the Role of the Oil Sector. *Comparative Economic Studies, 58*(1), 93–118. https://doi.org/10.1057/ces.2015.31

Kamp, M. (2009). Women's Studies and Gender Studies in Central Asia: Are We Talking to One Another. *Central Eurasian Studies Review, 8*(1), 2–12.

Kamp, M., & Nurdinova, S. (2022). Uzbek Migrants in Türkiye. *Region, 11*(2), 193–210.

Kim, S. (2023). Comparison of Happiness Levels in Central Asian Countries. *Journal of the Korea Society of Computer and Information, 28*(6), 145–152.

Kudebayeva, A., Sharipova, A., & Sharipova, D. (2022). Social Capital and Subjective Well-Being in Central Asia. *Europe-Asia Studies, 74*(1), 101–124. https://doi.org/10.1080/09668136.2021.1973965

Kuroki, M. (2011). Does Social Trust Increase Individual Happiness in Japan?*: M. Kuroki: Happiness and Trust. *Japanese Economic Review, 62*(4), 444–459. https://doi.org/10.1111/j.1468-5876.2011.00533.x

Laruelle, M., Huchet, J.-F., Peyrouse, S., & Balci, B. (2010). Why Central Asia? The Strategic Rationale of Indian and Chinese Involvement in the Region. In M. Laruelle, J.-F. Huchet, S. Peyrouse, & B. Balci (Eds.), *China and India in Central Asia* (pp. 1–6). Palgrave Macmillan US. https://doi.org/10.1057/9780230114357_1.

Li, J., Chen, Y., Li, Z., & Huang, X. (2019). Low-Carbon Economic Development in Central Asia Based on LMDI Decomposition and Comparative Decoupling Analyses. *Journal of Arid Land, 11*(4), 513–524. https://doi.org/10.1007/s40333-019-0063-0

"Life Expectancy at Birth of the Population of the Republic of Kazakhstan (2023)." (2023). https://stat.gov.kz/en/industries/social-statistics/demography/publications/157663/

Lu, H., Tong, P., & Zhu, R. (2020). Longitudinal Evidence on Social Trust and Happiness in China: Causal Effects and Mechanisms. *Journal of Happiness Studies, 21*, 1841–1858.

Luhmann, M., Hofmann, W., Eid, M., & Lucas, R. E. (2012). Subjective Well-Being and Adaptation to Life Events: A Meta-Analysis. *Journal of Personality and Social Psychology, 102*(3), 592.

Makulbayeva, G. A., Davletbayeva, Z. Z., & Dyussenov, M. M. (2023). Subjective Well-Being in Central Asia: Rural-Urban Differences, *145*(4), 363–373.

Marat, E. (2006). *The Tulip Revolution: Kyrgyzstan One Year After*. Jamestown Foundation Washington, DC. https://www.academia.edu/download/12961445/The_Tulip_Revolution.pdf

Marmot, M., & Bobak, M. (2005). Social and Economic Changes and Health in Europe East and West. *European Review, 13*(1), 15–31.

Matsushima, M., & Matsunaga, Y. (2015). Social Capital and Subjective Well-Being in Japan. *VOLUNTAS: International Journal of Voluntary and Nonprofit Organizations, 26*, 1016–1045.

McKee-Ryan, F., Song, Z., Wanberg, C. R., & Kinicki, A. J. (2005). Psychological and Physical Well-Being During Unemployment: A Meta-Analytic Study. *Journal of Applied Psychology, 90*(1), 53.

Meeks, R. (2012). *Culture and Gender Roles: Evidence from a Natural Experiment in Post-Soviet Central Asia*. https://www.dartmouth.edu/neudc2012/docs/paper_258.pdf

Megoran, N. (2010). The Uzbekistan-Kyrgyzstan Boundary: Stalin's Cartography, Post-Soviet Geography. In *Borderliness and Borderlands: Political Oddities at the Edge of the Nation-State* (pp. 33–52).

"Migration and Development Brief 38 | KNOMAD." (2023). https://knomad.org/publication/migration-and-development-brief-38

Myers, D. G. (2000). The Funds, Friends, and Faith of Happy People. *American Psychologist, 55*(1), 56.

Naghdi, Y., Amirtaemeh, H., & Kaghazian, S. (2021). The Puzzle of Relationship Between the Economic Growth and Happiness. *Economic Analysis, 54*(1), 1–12.

Neira Gómez, I., Lacalle-Calderon, M., Portela, M., & Pérez Trujillo, M. (n.d.). *Social Capital Dimensions and Subjective Wellbeing: A Quantile Approach.* https://minerva.usc.es/xmlui/handle/10347/32144. Accessed April 16, 2024.

Omarova, A., & Kenzhakimov, G. (2023). Sociological Measurement of the Happiness Index in Central Asian Countries. *Journal of Community Positive Practices, 1*, 17–28.

Oreopoulos, P. (2008). Priceless: The Nonpecuniary Benefits of Schooling. *Journal of Economic Perspectives, 25*(1), 1516.

Osmonova, D., Talgarbekova, E., Tashtanbekova, M., Moldoshova, A., & Anastassiadi, A. (2023). Evolution of Family Relationship in Kyrgyzstan. *Social and Legal Studios, 6*(4), 155–163.

"Population - Official Statistics - Statistics of the Kyrgyz Republic." (2024). https://stat.gov.kg/en/statistics/naselenie/

"Population of the Republic of Kazakhstan by Gender and Type of Locality (as of April 1, 2024)." (2024). https://stat.gov.kz/en/industries/social-statistics/demography/publications/159623/

Portela, M., Neira, I., & Del Mar Salinas-Jiménez, M. (2013). Social Capital and Subjective Well-being in Europe: A New Approach on Social Capital. *Social Indicators Research, 114*(2), 493–511. https://doi.org/10.1007/s11205-012-0158-x

Puntscher, S., Hauser, C., Walde, J., & Tappeiner, G. (2015). The Impact of Social Capital on Subjective Well-Being: A Regional Perspective. *Journal of Happiness Studies, 16*, 1231–1246.

Ram, R. (2010). Social Capital and Happiness: Additional Cross-Country Evidence. *Journal of Happiness Studies, 11*(4), 409–418. https://doi.org/10.1007/s10902-009-9148-3

Rosenfeld, M. J., & Roesler, K. (2019). Stability and Change in Predictors of Marital Dissolution in the US 1950–2015: The Rise of Family Inequality. In *Presented at the American Sociological Association Meetings in New York* [Google Scholar]. http://web.stanford.edu/~mrosenfe/Rosenfeld_and_Roesler_divorce_inequality.pdf

Ryff, C. D., & Boylan, J. M. (2016). Linking Happiness to Health: Comparisons between Hedonic and Eudaimonic Well-Being. *Handbook of Research Methods and Applications in Happiness and Quality of Life*, 53–70.

Selim, S. (2008). Life Satisfaction and Happiness in Turkey. *Social Indicators Research, 88*, 531–562.

Sen, A. (2006). Reason, Freedom and Well-Being. *Utilitas, 18*(1), 80–96.

Serikbayeva, B., & Abdulla, K. (2022). Good Governance Matters for Well-Being: The Case of Kazakhstan. *Transforming Government: People, Process and Policy, 16*(1), 140–164.

Sharipova, D., & Kudebayeva, A. (2023). Changing Well-Being in Central Asia: Evidence from Kazakhstan and Kyrgyzstan. *Journal of Happiness Studies, 24*(3), 1233–1260. https://doi.org/10.1007/s10902-022-00607-1

Spechler, M. C. (2008). The Economies of Central Asia: A Survey. *Comparative Economic Studies, 50*(1), 30–52. https://doi.org/10.1057/ces.2008.3

Suh, E., Diener, E., & Fujita, F. (1996). Events and Subjective Well-Being: Only Recent Events Matter. *Journal of Personality and Social Psychology, 70*(5), 1091.

Temirkulov, A. (2010). Kyrgyz 'Revolutions' in 2005 and 2010: Comparative Analysis of Mass Mobilization. *Nationalities Papers, 38*(5), 589–600.

Timur, D. (2006). Living Conditions, Intra-Societal Trust, and Public Concerns in Post-Socialist Turkmenistan. *Central Asia and the Caucasus, 4*(40), 122–132.

Tokhirov, A. (2023). *Income Fluctuations and Subjective Well-Being: Partially Mediating Effects of Remittances* (IOS Working Papers). https://www.econstor.eu/handle/10419/273577

Umberson, D., Williams, K., Powers, D. A., Chen, M. D., & Campbell, A. M. (2005). As Good as It Gets? A Life Course Perspective on Marital Quality. *Social Forces, 84*(1), 493–511.

United Nations. (2024). *Human Development Report 2023–24.* In *Human Development Reports.* United Nations. https://hdr.undp.org/content/human-development-report-2023-24

"Uzbekistan Pilot Multidimensional Poverty Index Report 2023: Poverty and Deprivation Analysis Using the Multidimensional Poverty Index (MPI) | OPHI." (2023). https://ophi.org.uk/publications/Uzbekistan-MPI-2023.

Veenhoven, R. (1984). The Concept of Happiness. In R. Veenhoven (Ed.), *Conditions of Happiness* (pp. 12–38). Springer Netherlands. https://doi.org/10.1007/978-94-009-6432-7_2.

Veenhoven, R. (2016). Quality of Life and Happiness: Concepts and Measures. In *Handbook of Research Methods and Applications in Happiness and Quality of Life* (pp. 309–333). Edward Elgar Publishing. https://www.elgaronline.com/abstract/edcoll/9781783471164/9781783471164.00020.xml

Waite, L., & Gallagher, M. (2001). *The Case for Marriage: Why Married People Are Happier, Healthier and Better off Financially*. Crown.

Welzel, C., & Inglehart, R. (2001). *Human Development and the" Explosion" of Democracy: Variations of Regime Change across 60 Societies*. https://www.ssoar.info/ssoar/handle/document/11513

Wilkinson, R. G., & Pickett, K. E. (2009). Income Inequality and Social Dysfunction. *Annual Review of Sociology, 35*(1), 493–511. https://doi.org/10.1146/annurev-soc-070308-115926

Winkelmann, R. (2009). Unemployment, Social Capital, and Subjective Well-Being. *Journal of Happiness Studies, 10*, 421–430.

"World Bank Open Data." (2024). *World Bank Open Data*. https://data.worldbank.org

Yamada, E., Shimizutani, S., & Murakami, E. (2022). Remittances, Household Welfare, and the COVID-19 Pandemic in Tajikistan. *Asian Development Review, 39*(02), 147–174. https://doi.org/10.1142/S0116110522500159

Chapter 5
Happiness and Social Norms in Central Asia

Abstract The social norms prevalent in Central Asia are deeply ingrained in the region's traditions, cultural practices, and historical experiences, influencing various facets of life such as family dynamics, gender roles, and community engagement. This chapter explores how these social norms shape perceptions of happiness, drawing from literature and empirical studies to provide a comprehensive understanding of the factors affecting subjective well-being in the region. By examining the interplay between social norms and happiness, this chapter aims to provide insights into the broader implications of these norms for individual and collective life satisfaction in Central Asia, shedding light on the complex relationship between cultural context and well-being in the region.

Keywords Social norms · Central Asia · Cultural traditions · Happiness · Subjective well-being · Gender roles

5.1 Introduction

Social norms are unwritten rules and expectations that govern behavior within a society. In Central Asia, social norms are deeply rooted in traditions, cultural practices, and historical experiences. These norms influence various aspects of life, including family dynamics, gender roles, and community engagement, all of which have implications for happiness and subjective well-being. Central Asian societies are often characterized by strong collectivist values. Collectivism emphasizes the importance of community and family over individual interests, fostering close-knit relationships and communal support systems (Hofstede, 2001). Traditional family structures and gender roles in Central Asia reflect a patriarchal orientation, where men are often seen as the primary breadwinners and where women are typically responsible for domestic roles (Kamp, 2009; Meeks, 2012) This chapter examines how social norms in Central Asia shape perceptions of happiness, drawing from literature and empirical studies, to offer a comprehensive understanding of the factors affecting subjective well-being in this region.

S. Nurdinova, *Happiness and Life Satisfaction in Central Asia*, Quality of Life in Asia 24, https://doi.org/10.1007/978-981-95-3082-3_5

Additionally, social norms in Central Asia impact community engagement and the nature of social support systems. In collectivist societies, community and familial ties are crucial for emotional and social support. The strong emphasis on communal values often results in networks of support and mutual aid, which can contribute positively to individuals' happiness. However, these same norms can also enforce conformity and limit personal autonomy, which may affect individual satisfaction differently depending on one's adherence to or deviation from these norms.

Understanding how social norms in Central Asia shape perceptions of happiness requires an examination of both empirical studies and theoretical perspectives. This chapter aims to offer a comprehensive understanding of how these norms influence subjective well-being in the region. By drawing on existing literature and empirical research, we will explore how traditional values, family dynamics, gender roles, and community engagement collectively impact happiness. This exploration will not only illuminate how social norms affect well-being but also provide insights into the broader implications of these norms for individual and collective life satisfaction in Central Asia.

The complex interplay between social norms and happiness in Central Asia emphasizes the importance of cultural context in shaping well-being. The region's collectivist values, traditional family structures, and gender roles all play a significant role in influencing how individuals experience and perceive happiness. By examining these factors, we can gain a deeper understanding of the factors affecting subjective well-being in Central Asia and appreciate the broader implications for social and psychological research.

5.2 National Identity and Happiness in Kazakhstan

Kazakhstan gained independence as a result of the dissolution of the Soviet Union in 1991, leading to substantial changes in national identity. The formation of an independent Kazakh country demanded the construction of a new national identity that distanced itself from Soviet legacies while embracing the country's historical, cultural, and ethnic uniqueness. This literature review analyzes the academic discussion concerning the transformations in Kazakh identity after the country gained independence. It specifically investigates the influence of the Soviet legacy, the government's initiatives in constructing a national identity, the reactions of society, and the manifestation of cultural expressions.

The Soviet period has dramatically influenced Kazakhstan's national identity. The USSR's policies aimed at building a cohesive Soviet identity, frequently at the cost of local identities. During the Soviet period, Kazakhstan experienced extensive Russification, which led to the dominance of Russian culture and language. This historical context is critical in understanding the dynamics of post-independence identity in Kazakhstan. The impact of Soviet intervention is notably evident in the demographic mix of Kazakhstan. At the time of independence, ethnic Kazakhs formed just a minority of the population, with considerable Russian, Ukrainian, and other ethnic groups (Smailov, 2000). The Soviet emphasis on industrialization and urbanization also contributed to a mixed ethnic milieu, complicating the process of building a unified national identity post-independence (Kesici, 2011).

After independence, Kazakhstan began nation-building initiatives aimed at forging a distinct national character. The government selected a multidimensional strategy, which included promoting Kazakh culture and language while preserving a narrative of multiculturalism and unity (Burkhanov, 2017). One of the significant foundations of Kazakhstan's nation-building efforts has been promoting the Kazakh language and culture. The government has enacted initiatives to revive and elevate the Kazakh language, which had been sidelined throughout the Soviet period. This effort may also be referred to as "Kazakhization." It involves initiatives such as establishing Kazakh as the state language, increasing its usage in government, education, and public life, and guaranteeing that it is taught as a first language in schools (Kesici, 2011; Toktarov et al., 2019).

Moreover, the strategic utilization of cultural manifestations, notably in music and visual arts, was central to promoting a united national identity. Kazakh music videos, for example, generally highlight traditional themes, presenting nomadic life and historical cultural traditions. These visual narratives connect current Kazakhs with their pre-Soviet heritage and provide an idealized image of nomadic practices in contrast to the repressive restrictions of the Soviet era. The incorporation of traditional Kazakh instruments in modern music emphasizes a deliberate attempt to bring back and honor pre-Soviet cultural traditions (Ifert Johnson, 2006). In line with cultural revival, the resurgence of Islam has become a key component of national identity in post-Soviet Kazakhstan. The state has actively encouraged the resurgence of Islamic practices and the construction of mosques, reflecting a more significant movement of recovering cultural and religious legacy that had been suppressed throughout the Soviet period (Yemelianova, 2013). Furthermore, sacred sites, such as mausoleums and pilgrimage destinations, have become vital national identity symbols, operating as focal areas for cultural preservation and social unity (Özkan et al., 2019). Additionally, horse culture, a sign of freedom and motion, and the nomadic tradition of the Kazakh people have been crucial to the state's nation-building activities (Sarbassova, 2015).

Civic nation-building has emerged as a significant subject in Kazakhstan's post-Soviet trajectory, to establish a shared "Kazakhstani" identity within its varied population. This strategy promotes common values, civic involvement, and a sense of belonging over ethnic or linguistic homogeneity (Schulz et al., 2018). However, the legacy of Soviet policy, especially concerning language and ethnicity, continues to impact identity dynamics. While the government promoted the Kazakh language as a unifying force, it also attempted to include sizable Russian-speaking minorities in the national fabric. This balancing act is evident in educational reforms, cultural initiatives, and public discourse, which seek to bridge potential differences and build a sense of a shared future. Nevertheless, the success of civic nation-building lies in managing the complexity of historical legacies, language policies, and the growing aspirations of Kazakhstan's varied population (Rees & Williams, 2017). Further research is vital to understanding how these elements impact the long-term evolution of national identity in Kazakhstan.

Kazakhstan's efforts in nation-building have also included policies addressing ethnic return migration, particularly the return of ethnic Kazakhs from abroad, known as "Oralmans." This effort intends to reinforce the ethnic Kazakh population within the country and strengthen Kazakh cultural and linguistic identity. The government has provided various incentives and support to facilitate the repatriation and integration of Oralmans into Kazakh society. This includes housing, schooling, employment support, and steps to ensure cultural and social assimilation. The strategy of ethnic return migration has prompted public controversy regarding its implications for social cohesion and the integration of other ethnic groups, highlighting the delicate balance between fostering Kazakh identity and maintaining a harmonious multiethnic society. Diener (2005) and Kuşçu (2013) studied the obstacles and complications of the Oralman program. While the Kazakh government wanted to bolster the titular population and counter emigration, both authors highlighted the gaps between this idealized vision and reality. Diener (2005) argues that inadequate settlement planning, limited government help, and discrepancies in legal frameworks produced considerable obstacles for Oralman in integrating into Kazakh society. This often led to disappointment and struggle for the returnees. Kuşçu (2013) adds to the issues associated with the inflow of Oralmen by investigating the public discourse around their entrance, emphasizing the socioeconomic strain placed on existing resources and the sense of discrimination against non-Kazakh ethnic groups. The integration of a vast number of individuals, many of whom arrived with minimal resources and linguistic barriers, posed considerable challenges in housing, jobs, and social services, straining Kazakhstan's social and economic institutions. This circumstance caused discontent among certain parts of the existing population, who felt that the government was prioritizing the interests of the newcomers over their own. Furthermore, the article (Kuşçu, 2013) illustrates how the preferential treatment granted to Oralman exacerbated notions of discrimination against non-Kazakh ethnic groups within Kazakhstan, raising concerns about the influence of such policies on interethnic relations and national unity.

While fostering Kazakh identity, the government has also highlighted the need for ethnic peace and pluralism. Kazakhstan is home to approximately 130 ethnic groups, making the management of ethnic relations an essential component of nation-building. The formation of the Assembly of the People of Kazakhstan in 1995 illustrates this devotion. The Assembly functions as a consultative body aimed at strengthening interethnic discussion and collaboration. It comprises representatives from diverse ethnic communities, offering a platform for expressing their views and encouraging cultural interchange. The Assembly serves a symbolic function in fostering the notion of a single Kazakhstani identity that incorporates all ethnic groups within the nation. However, its usefulness in tackling more profound structural inequality and political representation remains contested. Critics claim that while the Assembly fosters interethnic cooperation on a symbolic level, it lacks substantial political authority and impact (Burkhanov, 2018).

Despite attempts to separate Kazakhstan from its Soviet past, the legacy of the Soviet Union nevertheless shapes national identity. From the Russian language's persistent presence to the ongoing usage of Soviet-era infrastructure and organizations, Kazakh society has exhibited Soviet influence in many spheres. Integrating its Soviet past into a new national narrative that prioritizes Kazakh cultural and historical components has presented difficulty for Kazakhstan. The Soviet legacy remains in the political and administrative systems of Kazakhstan. Many government officials and bureaucrats were educated in Soviet institutions, so the centralized governance model captures Soviet administrative methods. This continuity highlights the difficulty of creating a new national identity without breaking away from the Soviet past (Burkhanov, 2018) (Table 5.1).

The average happiness score in Wave 6 was approximately 3.20 on a 1–4 scale, with a standard deviation of 0.63. The average happiness score in Wave 7 is slightly higher at 3.24, with a standard deviation of 0.60. The reduced standard deviation suggests a slightly more consistent perception of happiness compared with Wave 6.

In Wave 6, the average life satisfaction score was 7.26 on a 1–10 scale, with a standard deviation of 2.10. This indicates a relatively high level of life satisfaction among respondents, although there is substantial variability in life satisfaction levels. The average life satisfaction score in Wave 7 was slightly lower at 7.14, with a standard deviation of 2.04. The decrease in the standard deviation indicates a reduction in variability in life satisfaction compared with that in Wave 6.

The mean value of 0.40 suggests that approximately 40% of the respondents are male. In Wave 7, the mean is 0.45, indicating a slight increase in the proportion of male respondents to 45%, with a similar level of variability in the gender distribution.

The average age of the respondents in Wave 6 was 40.11 years, with a standard deviation of 15.47 years. This suggests a broad age range among participants, from young adults to those in their late 80s. In Wave 7, the average age increases slightly to 41.88 years, with a reduced standard deviation of 13.87 years, indicating a somewhat narrower age distribution than that in Wave 6.

In both waves, the mean values indicate that approximately 63% to 68% of the respondents are employed, with a similar level of variability in employment status. The low mean values suggest that a small percentage of respondents (6 and 5%) are unemployed, with a slight decrease in Wave 7. Approximately 30% of the respondents were out of the labor force in Wave 6, with a slight decrease in Wave 7 (27%). The proportion of single respondents was approximately 20% in Wave 6 and decreased to 13% in Wave 7. The proportion of married respondents was approximately 82% in Wave 6 and decreased to 68% in Wave 7. Approximately 18% of the respondents were divorced in both waves.

The means and standard deviations for these variables indicate the average level of importance respondents place on each aspect on a 1–4 scale. For example, "Important: Family" has an average mean close to 1.08, indicating that family is highly valued on average, with a standard deviation reflecting variability in responses. "Important: Politics" and "Important: Religion" have moderate levels of importance, with standard deviations suggesting varying degrees of emphasis among respondents. The

Table 5.1 Variable definitions

Variable	Definition
Life satisfaction	All things considered, how satisfied are you with your life as a whole these days? (1 = completely dissatisfied to 10 = completely satisfied)
Happiness	Taking all things together, would you say you are? (1 = not at all happy, 2 = not very happy, 3 = rather happy, 4 = very happy)
Age	Your age in years
Gender	0 typically represents female respondents, 1 typically represents male respondents
Employment status	Employment status is likely represented as a set of dummy variables. "Out of labor market" refers to retired/pensioned, homemaker not otherwise employed, and student. "Unemployed" refers to individuals who are currently not employed but actively seeking employment. "Employed" refers to full-time (30 h a week or more), part-time (less than 30 h a week), and self-employed
Married, single, divorced	Marital status is represented as a set of dummy variables, where each category of marital status (e.g., married, single, divorced) is coded as 1 or 0
Important: family	Importance of family in life (1 = very important, 4 = not at all important)
Important: politics	Importance of politics in life (1 = very important, 4 = not at all important)
Important: friends	Importance of friends in life (1 = very important, 4 = not at all important)
Important: leisure	Importance of leisure in life (1 = very important, 4 = not at all important)
Important: religion	Importance of religion in life (1 = very important, 4 = not at all important)
Important: work	Importance of work in life (1 = very important, 4 = not at all important)
Government's responsibility	(1 = The government should take more responsibility, 10 = The government should not take responsibility)
Political scale	Self-positioning on the political scale (1 = left, 10 = right)
Confidence: government	Confidence in the government (1 = a great deal, 4 = not at all)
Political system	To what extent, in your opinion, are the opinions of people like you taken into account by the political system when making important government decisions? (1 = a great deal, 4 = not at all)
Vote in national elections	Frequency of voting in national elections (1 = always, 4 = not at all)
Democratic system	Belief that governments should tax the rich and subsidize the poor (1 = not an essential characteristic of democracy, 10 = essential characteristic of democracy)
Secure in neighborhood	Feeling of security in your neighborhood (1 = very secure, 4 = not very secure at all)
Trust	Belief that most people can be trusted (0 = no, 1 = yes)
Parents' proud	One of the main goals in life has been to make my parents proud (1 = strongly agree, 4 = strongly disagree)
National proud	How proud you are of your nationality (1 = very proud, 5 = not at all nationalist)
Men as political leaders	Belief that men make better political leaders than women (1 = agree strongly, 4 = disagree strongly)
Jobs scarce	Belief that men should have more rights to a job than women (1 = agree strongly, 5 = disagree strongly)

mean value increases from 1.73 in Wave 6 to 2.14 in Wave 7, indicating a perceived increase in neighborhood security.

The proportion of respondents who trusted others was lower in Wave 7, reflecting a decrease in the average level of trust. This variable measures the degree of pride respondents feel from their parents, with an average score of 1.52 indicating a moderate level of pride. The mean value of 1.45 suggests a moderate level of national pride among respondents.

The mean indicates moderate support for men as political leaders, with a slight increase in Wave 7 (Mean = 2.3270). The mean value increases from 1.85 to 2.56, suggesting that respondents in Wave 7 perceive jobs to be scarcer than those in Wave 6 do (Table 5.2).

The table shows the regression results for happiness and life satisfaction in Kazakhstan. The Wave 6 study examined various factors and their associations with life satisfaction and happiness. The variables considered in the study include gender, age, employment status, marital status, and the importance of family, friends, leisure, politics, work, religion, neighborhood security, trust, national pride, and perceptions of men as political leaders and job scarcity.

Age is negatively associated with both life satisfaction and happiness, with coefficients of −0.014 and −0.005, respectively. The negative association is stronger for life satisfaction, and the significance level is greater for happiness. This suggests a similar negative effect of age on happiness, where older individuals report slightly lower happiness.

Being employed is negatively associated with happiness, with a coefficient of −0.15. This suggests that being employed is linked to lower levels of happiness than being out of labor.

Conversely, being unemployed is even more strongly negatively associated with both life satisfaction and happiness, with coefficients of −0.83 and −0.20, respectively. This indicates a substantial negative impact on life satisfaction and happiness for those who are unemployed.

Being single is negatively associated with happiness, with the coefficient being −0.09. This suggests that being single is linked to lower levels of happiness than being in the reference group. Being divorced is strongly negatively associated with both life satisfaction and happiness, with coefficients of −0.77 and −0.23, respectively. This indicates a substantial negative impact on life satisfaction and happiness for those who are divorced.

The importance of placing one's family in one's life is negatively associated with happiness, with a coefficient of −0.16. This suggests that valuing one's family is linked to greater happiness. The importance of placing on friends is negatively associated with happiness, with coefficients of −0.07. This finding indicates that valuing friends is linked to higher levels of happiness. The importance of work is positively associated with life satisfaction, indicating that work is less important for increasing life satisfaction. The variable secure in the neighborhood is negatively associated with both life satisfaction and happiness, with coefficients of −0.21 and −0.07, respectively.

Table 5.2 Descriptive statistics

Variable	Wave 6: Mean	Wave 6: Std. Dev	Wave 7: Mean	Wave 7: Std. Dev	Min	Max
Happiness	3.20	0.63	3.24	0.60	1	4
Life satisfaction	7.26	2.10	7.14	2.04	1	10
Gender	0.40	0.49	0.45	0.50	0	1
Age	40.11	15.47	41.88	13.87	18	88
Employed	0.63	0.48	0.68	0.47	0	1
Unemployed	0.06	0.24	0.05	0.22	0	1
Out of labor	0.30	0.46	0.27	0.45	0	1
Single	0.20	0.40	0.13	0.34	0	1
Married	0.82	0.38	0.68	0.47	0	1
Divorced	0.18	0.38	0.19	0.39	0	1
Important: family	1.08	0.30	1.07	0.28	1	4
Important: friends	1.66	0.74	1.74	0.74	1	4
Important: leisure	1.80	0.81	1.84	0.80	1	4
Important: politics	2.58	0.87	2.56	0.92	1	4
Important: work	1.59	0.85	1.63	0.77	1	4
Important: religion	2.34	0.94	2.07	0.92	1	4
Secure in neighborhood	1.73	0.74	2.14	0.72	1	4
Trust	0.39	0.49	0.25	0.43	0	1
Parents' proud			1.52	0.64	1	4
National proud	1.45	0.65			1	5
Men as political leaders	2.17	0.95	2.33	0.86	1	4
Jobs scarce	1.85	0.84	2.56	1.18	1	3
N	1452		789			

Trust has a positive effect on life satisfaction. National pride is negatively associated with both life satisfaction and happiness, with coefficients of −0.5 and −0.19, respectively. This finding indicates that higher levels of national pride are linked to higher levels of life satisfaction and happiness.

If there is job scarcity, men should have more rights to jobs, resulting in a relatively weaker association with happiness (Table 5.3).

Table 5.3 Values and subjective well-being

Variable	Wave 6: life satisfaction	Wave 6: happiness	Wave 7: life satisfaction	Wave 7: happiness
Gender	−0.03	−0.01	−0.25	−0.05
Age	−0.01**	−0.00***	−0.01	−0.00
Employed	−0.12	−0.15***	0.43	0.07
Unemployed	−0.83**	−0.20**	(Omitted)	(Omitted)
Out of labor	(Omitted)	(Omitted)	0.19	0.06
Single	−0.26	−0.09*	0.00	0.03
Married	(Omitted)	(Omitted)	0.07	0.04
Divorced	−0.77***	−0.23***	(Omitted)	(Omitted)
Important: family	0.21	−0.16*	−0.36	−0.05
Important: friends	−0.15	−0.07**	−0.37***	−0.04
Important: leisure	−0.02	0.01	0.13	0.02
Important: politics	−0.07	−0.03	0.06	0.00
Important: work	0.18*	0.00	0.06	−0.04
Important: religion	0.05	−0.00	−0.39***	−0.02
Secure in neighborhood	−0.21**	−0.07**	−0.43***	−0.14***
Trust	0.23*	0.05	0.30	0.15**
Parents' proud	(Omitted)	(Omitted)	−0.59***	−0.18***
National proud	−0.50***	−0.19***	(Omitted)	(Omitted)
Men as political leaders	0.03	0.03	−0.11	−0.01
Jobs scarce	0.10	−0.04*	−0.09	0.01
Constant	8.78***	4.34***	10.75***	3.87***
N	1452	1452	789	789
R^2	0.09	0.14	0.16	0.09

Legend *$p < 0.05$; **$p < 0.01$; ***$p < 0.001$

The results from Wave 7 of the study provide insights into the factors influencing life satisfaction and happiness. Most sociodemographic variables have insignificant impacts on both life satisfaction and happiness. The coefficient is −0.37, which is significant at the 0.001 level. Valuing friends also correlates with higher life satisfaction. The coefficient is −0.39, which is significant at the 0.001 level. The importance of placing on religion is associated with significantly increased life satisfaction. With a coefficient of 0.15, trust positively influences happiness.

Feeling secure in one's neighborhood is negatively associated with happiness and life satisfaction, indicating that greater security increases both life satisfaction and happiness.

One of the main goals in life has been to make one's parents proud, which has a negative effect on both happiness and life satisfaction. Those who do not agree that one's parents are proud have lower happiness and life satisfaction.

In conclusion, the transformation of Kazakhstan's national identity post-independence has been a multifaceted process influenced by the legacy of the Soviet Union, government initiatives, societal reactions, and cultural expressions. The Soviet era's Russification policies and demographic changes significantly shaped the initial challenges faced in forging a new national identity. In response, the Kazakh government has undertaken comprehensive nation-building efforts, emphasizing the revival of the Kazakh language and culture, promoting ethnic return migration, and fostering civic nation-building. These initiatives aim to construct a cohesive national identity that honors Kazakhstan's historical, cultural, and ethnic uniqueness while striving to maintain ethnic peace and pluralism. The resurgence of Islam, cultural revitalization, and strategic utilization of cultural manifestations have been central to these efforts. However, the integration of *oralmans* and the balancing of ethnic relations highlight the complexities and challenges inherent in this process. As Kazakhstan continues to navigate its post-Soviet trajectory, further research is essential to understand the long-term impacts of these nation-building strategies on evolving national identity. This literature review emphasizes the dynamic interplay between historical legacies and contemporary policies in shaping the national identity of Kazakhstan, revealing both the progress made and the challenges that remain.

5.3 Values and Life Satisfaction in Kyrgyzstan

As Kyrgyzstan continues to navigate its post-Soviet transition and embrace modernization, the relationship between values and life satisfaction has become an important area of study. Values, which encompass the principles and beliefs that guide individuals' behaviors and judgments, play a crucial role in shaping overall life satisfaction. This chapter explores the connection between values and life satisfaction in Kyrgyzstan, drawing on empirical research, cultural insights, and theoretical frameworks to provide a comprehensive analysis.

Research indicates that family and community values significantly contribute to life satisfaction in Kyrgyzstan. A study by Osmonova et al. (2023) highlighted that strong family bonds and community support systems are associated with higher levels of life satisfaction (Table 5.4).

The mean happiness score in wave 6 was 3.32, with a standard deviation of 0.55, whereas in wave 4, it was 3.05, with a standard deviation of 0.60. Similarly, the mean life satisfaction score in wave 6 was 6.93, with a standard deviation of 2.16, whereas in wave 4, it was 6.55, with a standard deviation of 2.56. The mean financial satisfaction was greater in wave 6 (6.36, standard deviation 2.34) than in wave 4 (5.73, std. dev. 2.57). The mean number of children and health status seemed to have changed between the two waves, with different standard deviations as well. The gender distribution appeared to have shifted slightly, with the mean for gender

Table 5.4 Variable definitions

Variable	Definition
Life satisfaction	Overall satisfaction with life, rated from 1 (completely dissatisfied) to 10 (completely satisfied)
Happiness	General happiness, where 1 = not at all happy, 2 = not very happy, 3 = rather happy, and 4 = very happy
Financial satisfaction	Satisfaction with household financial situation, where 1 = completely dissatisfied and 10 = completely satisfied
Number of children	The total number of children the respondent has
Health status	Subjective health status, rated from 1 (very good) to 5 (very poor)
Gender	Gender of the respondent, where 0 = female and 1 = male
Age	Age of the respondent in years
Married, single, divorced	Marital status represented by dummy variables: 1 indicates the category (married, single, or divorced) and 0 indicates not in that category
Proud of nationality	Level of pride in nationality, where 1 = very proud and 5 = not at all proud
Importance: family	Importance of family in the respondent's life, rated from 1 (very important) to 4 (not at all important)
Importance: friends	Importance of friends in the respondent's life, rated from 1 (very important) to 4 (not at all important)
Importance: god	Importance of God in the respondent's life, where 1 = not at all important and 10 = very important
Importance: work	Importance of work in the respondent's life, rated from 1 (very important) to 4 (not at all important)
Importance: religion	Importance of religion in the respondent's life, rated from 1 (very important) to 4 (not at all important)
Men/women as political leaders	Perception of whether men make better political leaders than women, where 1 = agree strongly and 4 = disagree strongly
Men/women as business executives	Perception of whether men make better business executives than women, where 1 = agree strongly and 4 = disagree strongly
Jobs scarce: men's rights	Opinion on whether men should have more rights to jobs than women when jobs are scarce, where 1 = agree strongly and 5 = disagree strongly
Employment status	Employment status represented by dummy variables: 1 indicates the category (employed, unemployed, or out of the labor market) and 0 indicates not in that category
Education level	The highest level of education completed by the respondent, ranging from early childhood education (0) to the highest level achieved
Age Sqr	The square of the respondent's age, calculated by multiplying the age by itself
Income scale	Household income level on a scale from 1 (lowest income) to 10 (highest income)

being 0.49 in wave 6 and 0.44 in wave 4. In Wave 6, the mean age was approximately 38.80 years, with a standard deviation of approximately 14.28 (Table 5.5).

In Wave 4, the mean age was slightly lower at approximately 37.16 years, with a standard deviation of approximately 15.35. The data indicate that in Wave 6, the proportion of individuals who were married was approximately 76.20%, with a standard deviation of approximately 42.60%. In Wave 4, the proportion of married individuals decreased to approximately 62.21%, with a standard deviation of approximately 48.51%. The proportion of single individuals increased from approximately 15.50% in Wave 6 to approximately 24.73% in Wave 4, with corresponding standard deviations.

Table 5.6 presents the regression results for the relationships between various social factors and life satisfaction and happiness in Kyrgyzstan across the two waves.

Table 5.5 Descriptive statistics

Variable	Wave 6: Mean	Wave 6: Std. Dev	Wave 4: Mean	Wave 4: Std. Dev	Min	Max
Happiness	3.32	0.55	3.05	0.60	1	4
Life satisfaction	6.93	2.16	6.55	2.56	1	10
Financial satisfaction	6.36	2.34	5.73	2.57	1	10
Number of children	2.37	1.79	2.07	1.92	0	8
Health	2.09	0.71	2.31	0.76	1	4
Gender	0.49	0.50	0.44	0.50	0	1
Age	38.80	14.28	37.16	15.35	18	89
Married	0.76	0.43	0.62	0.49	0	1
Single	0.16	0.36	0.25	0.43	0	1
Divorced	0.08	0.28	0.15	0.35	0	1
Proud of nationality	1.50	0.63	1.79	0.84	1	5
Importance: family	1.04	0.20	1.13	0.36	1	3
Importance: friends	1.79	0.61	1.60	0.66	1	4
Importance: god	8.34	2.27	7.79	2.77	1	10
Men better political leader	2.21	0.89	2.37	0.93	1	4
Men more right at job	1.79	0.81	1.89	0.94	1	3
Education	6.79	1.92	6.70	1.92	1	9
N	1374		942			

Table 5.6 Social factors of subjective well-being

Variable	Wave 6: life satisfaction	Wave 6: happiness	Wave 4: happiness	Wave 4: life satisfaction
Financial Satisfaction	0.33***	0.03***	0.04***	0.61***
Number of children	−0.00	0.01	0.03*	0.14**
Health	−0.29***	−0.26***	−0.27***	−0.22**
Gender	−0.12	−0.04	−0.03	0.10
Age	0.01	−0.00	−0.00	−0.01*
Married	−0.24	0.07	0.19	0.16
Single	(Omitted)	(Omitted)	0.18	0.09
Divorced	−0.74**	−0.10	−0.00	−0.50
Proud of nationality	−0.14	−0.11***	−0.07**	−0.03
Importance: family	−0.13	−0.06	−0.08	0.09
Importance: friends	0.07	−0.03	−0.03	−0.23*
Importance: god	0.15***	−0.01	0.01	0.02
Men better political leader	0.13*	0.01	0.01	0.17*
Men more right at job	0.07	0.00	−0.04*	0.02
Education	0.02	−0.02**	−0.02*	0.02
Constant	3.87***	4.13***	3.68***	3.33***
N	1374	1374	942	942
R^2	0.21	0.18	0.26	0.47

Legend $*p < 0.05$; $**p < 0.01$; $***p < 0.001$

Financial satisfaction has a significant positive effect on both happiness and life satisfaction in Wave 6, as indicated by the coefficients of 0.33 and 0.61, respectively. These coefficients suggest that an increase in financial satisfaction is associated with higher levels of happiness and life satisfaction. This aligns with the findings of Easterlin (2001) and Diener et al. (1999) that financial stability is crucial for subjective well-being.

Health has a strong negative effect on both happiness and life satisfaction in both waves. The coefficients indicate that better health is associated with higher levels of happiness and life satisfaction. Ryff and Boylan (2016) highlighted that health is a foundational element of well-being, making its deterioration a significant concern. Being divorced has a notably negative effect on life satisfaction in Wave 6. The negative effect of divorce on life satisfaction aligns with that of Umberson et al. (2005), who reported that changes in marital status can significantly affect well-being. The results suggest that support systems and social integration are crucial for those who are divorced.

The results show a minimal impact of the number of children on well-being, which might differ from studies such as (Rosenfeld & Roesler, 2019). This discrepancy could be due to cultural differences or varying economic pressures in Kyrgyzstan.

The regression analysis highlights the critical role of financial satisfaction, health, and religion in determining subjective well-being in Kyrgyzstan. The results align with much of the literature but also reflect unique contextual factors. Future research should continue to explore these dynamics and consider additional variables and cultural contexts to further understand the complex relationships between social factors and subjective well-being in Kyrgyzstan.

5.4 Gender Norms and Happiness in Tajikistan

Social norms in Tajikistan place significant emphasis on achieving success, particularly in terms of education, employment, and economic status. Gender norms in Tajikistan, which are influenced by historical, cultural, and religious factors, significantly impact the subjective well-being of its citizens. Tajikistan society is predominantly patriarchal, with men traditionally seen as the primary breadwinners and decision-makers (Falkingham, 2000; Harris, 2000). Women's roles are often confined to domestic duties, including childcare and household management. This chapter provides a comprehensive overview of how gender norms in Tajikistan influence happiness, highlighting the importance of the cultural context in understanding well-being (Table 5.7).

This table provides descriptive statistics for various variables measured in a survey dataset, offering insights into their distribution and central tendencies among Tajikistan people. The average reported level of happiness among respondents is 3.56 (on a scale from 1 to 4), with a standard deviation of 0.61, indicating moderate variability in happiness levels across the sample. On average, the respondents reported a life satisfaction score of 7.93 (on a scale from 1 to 10), with a standard deviation of 1.85. This suggests a wider range of satisfaction levels among individuals, reflecting diverse perceptions of overall quality of life. The respondents reported an average of approximately 3.34 children per household, with a standard deviation of 1.81. This indicates variability in family sizes within the sample, ranging from no children to as many as 13. The importance of the family was rated on average at 1.04 (on a scale from 1 to 3), with a standard deviation of 0.20. The respondents rated the importance of friends at an average of 1.59 (on a scale from 1 to 4), with a standard deviation of 0.67. Leisure activities were rated with an average importance of 2.15 (on a scale from 1 to 4), with a standard deviation of 0.90. The importance of politics was rated on average at 2.33 (on a scale from 1 to 4), with a standard deviation of 0.95. The respondents rated the importance of work at an average of 1.58 (on a scale from 1 to 4), with a standard deviation of 0.78. Religion was rated with an average importance of 1.52 (on a scale from 1 to 4), with a standard deviation of 0.72. Among the respondents, 94.23% reported being married, 0.31% reported being single, and 5.46% reported being divorced, reflecting the marital composition within the sample.

Table 5.7 Variable definitions

Variable	Definition
Life satisfaction	All things considered, how satisfied are you with your life as a whole these days? (1 = Completely dissatisfied, 10 = Completely satisfied)
Happiness	Taking all things together, would you say you are: (1 = Not at all happy, 2 = Not very happy, 3 = Rather happy, 4 = Very happy)
Number of children	How many children do you have?
Important: family	How important is family in your life? (1 = Very important, 4 = Not at all important)
Important: friends	How important are friends in your life? (1 = Very important, 4 = Not at all important)
Important: leisure	How important is leisure in your life? (1 = Very important, 4 = Not at all important)
Important: politics	How important is politics in your life? (1 = Very important, 4 = Not at all important)
Important: work	How important is work in your life? (1 = Very important, 4 = Not at all important)
Important: religion	How important is religion in your life? (1 = Very important, 4 = Not at all important)
Marital status	Marital status represented as dummy variables: (1 = Married, 0 = Not married), (1 = Single, 0 = Not single), (1 = Divorced, 0 = Not divorced)
Employment status	Employment status represented as dummy variables: (1 = Employed, 0 = Not employed), (1 = Unemployed, 0 = Not unemployed), (1 = Out of labor market, 0 = Not out of labor market)
Education level	Highest educational level: 0 = Early childhood education, up to the highest level of education
Age	Age in years
Men/women as political leaders	Do you agree that men make better political leaders than women? (1 = Agree strongly, 4 = Disagree strongly)
Men/women as business executives	Do you agree that men make better business executives than women? (1 = Agree strongly, 4 = Disagree strongly)
Jobs scarce: men's rights	Do you agree that men should have more rights to a job than women when jobs are scarce? (1 = Agree strongly, 5 = Disagree strongly)
Women's income problem	Do you agree that it is a problem if women earn more income than their husband? (1 = Agree strongly, 5 = Disagree strongly)

Approximately 45.33% of the respondents were employed, 24.76% were unemployed, and 29.91% were out of the labor force, indicating the distribution of employment statuses among the sample population. The average education level among the respondents was 4.28 (on a scale from 0 to 8), with a standard deviation of 1.88. The average age of the respondents was 44.23 years, with a standard deviation of

13.68, ranging from 18 to 83 years. This indicates a diverse age distribution within the sample, reflecting different life stages and generational perspectives. On average, the respondents rated men/women as political leaders at 1.93 and men/women as business executives at 2.12 (on a scale from 1 to 4), indicating perceptions of gender roles and representation in leadership positions. The respondents rated issues related to job scarcity and women's income problems at averages of 2.34 and 2.79, respectively (on scales from 1 to 5), reflecting perceptions of gender disparities in the workforce and income equality challenges (Table 5.8).

The table shows a detailed interpretation of the regression analysis for life satisfaction and happiness on the basis of the provided data. Variables such as the number of children and the importance of family status have statistically insignificant impacts on both life satisfaction and happiness (Table 5.9).

There is a statistically significant negative effect of the importance of friends on life satisfaction, with a coefficient of −0.23. This suggests that placing greater importance on friendships may increase overall life satisfaction. The importance of work has a statistically significant negative effect on life satisfaction, with a coefficient of −0.19.

Table 5.8 Descriptive statistics

Variable	Mean	Std. Dev	Min	Max
Happiness	3.56	0.61	1	4
Life satisfaction	7.93	1.85	1	10
Number of children	3.34	1.81	0	13
Important: family	1.04	0.20	1	3
Important: friends	1.59	0.67	1	4
Important: leisure	2.15	0.90	1	4
Important: politics	2.33	0.95	1	4
Important: work	1.58	0.78	1	4
Important: religion	1.52	0.72	1	4
Single	0.00	0.06	0	1
Married	0.94	0.23	0	1
Divorced	0.05	0.23	0	1
Employed	0.45	0.50	0	1
Unemployed	0.25	0.43	0	1
Out of labor	0.30	0.46	0	1
Education level	4.28	1.88	0	8
Age	44.23	13.68	18	83
Men/women as political leaders	1.93	1.00	1	4
Men/women as business executives	2.12	1.03	1	4
Jobs scarce: men's rights	2.34	1.33	1	5
Women's income problem	2.79	1.38	1	5
N	953			

Table 5.9 Gender norms and subjective well-being

Variable	Life satisfaction	Happiness
Number of children	0.07	0.01
Important: family	0.27	0.12
Important: friends	−0.23**	−0.08*
Important: leisure	−0.09	−0.04
Important: politics	−0.12	−0.03
Important: work	−0.20*	−0.06*
Important: religion	−0.00	−0.06*
Single	1.73	0.67***
Married	1.19***	0.30*
Divorced	(Omitted)	(Omitted)
Employed	0.29	0.02
Unemployed	(Omitted)	(Omitted)
Out of labor	0.32	0.05
Education level	−0.01	−0.01
Age	−0.00	0.00
Men/women as political leaders	0.03	−0.03
Men/women as business executives	0.09	−0.02
Jobs scarce: men's rights	−0.12*	−0.00
Women's income problem	0.19***	0.02
Constant	6.90***	3.66***
N	953	953
R^2	0.08	0.06

Legend *$p < 0.05$; **$p < 0.01$; ***$p < 0.001$

This finding indicates that individuals who prioritize work-related achievements and career success tend to report higher levels of life satisfaction. The importance of religion, leisure, and politics has no statistically significant effect on life satisfaction. Being married has a statistically significant positive effect on life satisfaction, with a coefficient of 1.19. The employment status, educational level, age and gender perceptions of men as political leaders and business executives have no significant impact on life satisfaction. People who consider that men should have more right to a job than women in job-scarce cases are more satisfied with their lives (−0.12). People who do not consider a problem if women have more income than husbands are more satisfied with their lives than those who consider it a problem.

For happiness, there is a statistically insignificant effect of the importance of leisure and politics on happiness. The importance of work and religion has a statistically significant effect on happiness, with a coefficient of −0.06. This suggests that individuals who prioritize work and religion tend to report higher levels of happiness, benefiting from emotional support and relational fulfillment. Being single or married has a statistically significant positive effect on happiness, with coefficients of 0.67 and 0.30, respectively. Single individuals report significantly higher levels of happiness than other marital statuses do, possibly due to greater personal freedom and independence.

5.5 Social Capital and Life Satisfaction in Uzbekistan

There has been a growing body of scholarship regarding happiness economics since the 1980s, which has constituted social capital as a determinant of happiness. Social capital is defined as the norms, rules, networks, communications, and mutual trust that affect the economic development of societies. According to Bourdieu, social capital is "the sum of the resources, actual or virtual, that accrue to an individual or a group by possessing a durable network of more or less institutionalized relationships of mutual acquaintance and recognition" (Gauntlett, 2018). As trust, networks, and norms are the key pillars of social capital, numerous studies concentrate more on one or more of these three dimensions, with generalized trust measures being among the variables that are most commonly utilized.

Research on social capital indicates that it plays a significant role in determining subjective well-being. Subjective well-being was defined as "people's cognitive and affective evaluations of their lives" by Diener (2000). In this study, happiness, life satisfaction, and subjective well-being are used interchangeably. According to Veenhoven, happiness is defined as "the degree to which an individual judges the overall quality of his life-as-a-whole favorably" (Veenhoven, 1984).

Subjective well-being can be impacted differently by elements of social capital such as institutions, networks, and trust. Some studies show that certain countries are happier than others; specifically, developed countries such as the Netherlands, Switzerland, and Iceland have the highest level of social capital and happiness score, whereas the reverse is true for low-income countries. Additionally, generalized trust has a positive effect on national happiness (Bjørnskov, 2003). Matsushima and Matsunaga emphasized that trusting people are more likely to report higher happiness levels. However, the authors' findings revealed that there was no statistically significant difference in reported happiness between untrusting individuals and "trust-neutral individuals" (Matsushima & Matsunaga, 2015). In terms of both institutional and general trust, the empirical data regarding the effects of these social capital components on the regional level of life satisfaction showed distinctly positive coefficients (Puntscher et al., 2015). A recent study on Türkiye has shown that trust plays a significant role in predicting happiness and life satisfaction, whereas generalized trust was a predictor in 2008, which was not the case in 1999. The results suggest that social, cultural, and political transformations that occurred between 2000 and 2008, including an economic crisis in 2001, Europeanization processes, and the emphasis on Islamic values by the ruling political party, may have played a role in this change (Ekici & Koydemir, 2014). While social capital was estimated in high- and low-income economies, the association of trust with life satisfaction was significant in the top halves. Nevertheless, the authors considered that social capital was a critical factor for happiness, even at lower income levels. For example, in the case of Latin America, the social capital embodied in the structure of families and communities plays a vital role in driving higher-than-predicted happiness levels (Ram, 2010). Another study highlighted the role of human, economic, social, and psychological capital in determining life satisfaction during the pandemic in Germany and the United Kingdom. The authors found that psychological capital was the strongest predictor of life satisfaction, approximately four times as high as social capital. These results suggest that weathering during the pandemic first required psychological resources (Delhey et al., 2023).

The causality between social capital and subjective well-being was estimated in the case of China. Random effects instrumental variable and two-stage residual inclusion estimates have shown that social trust has a positive causal effect on individual happiness. A significant cross-level interaction effect between individual trust and aggregate social trust was also found, indicating that the happiness of those with low individual trust is more likely to be impacted by social trust (Lu et a., 2020) Using the German Socioeconomic Panel, Winkelmann's (2009) study supported the literature on social capital and revealed that attendance at activities had a positive and statistically significant effect on subjective well-being. In particular, the models for female participants revealed the largest effect from the attendance of cultural events and sports (Winkelmann, 2009). Another study reported that there was a positive effect between feelings of social affiliation and subjective well-being. Feelings of social affiliation mediated 32.5% of the overall impact of social capital on subjective well-being, suggesting a relationship between feelings of belonging to the social whole and trust in social networks (Hommerich & Tiefenbach, 2018). The importance of social capital was supported by Portela and her coauthors (Portela et al., 2013). Their findings showed that social networks, social trust, and institutional trust are the components that have a greater correlation with subjective well-being. Formal networks have little impact on life happiness, whereas participation in political networks has no significant effect on any component of subjective well-being. Yanjie Bian and coauthors also reported that formal networks, which include participation in political and social organizations, have less impact than does social contact with relatives and friends (Bian et al., 2018). In contrast, in the USA case, people who are more satisfied with their lives are more likely to vote. Several political engagement activities were substantially associated with life happiness, and the degree of this association was equivalent to or greater than that of other common participation predictors (Flavin & Keane, 2012).

The happiness of the least happy individuals can increase more easily than that of the happiest individuals by improving their trustworthiness and participating more in social networks or civic engagement actions (Neira Gómez et al., n.d.).

Noneconomic factors such as social trust can be strong predictors of changes in subjective well-being over time in the medium term in transition countries (Bartolini et al., 2017) (Table 5.10).

The survey questions specifically ask, "Taking all things together, would you say you are (1) very happy (2) rather happy (3) not very happy (4) not at all happy" and

Table 5.10 Variable definitions

Variable	Definition
Happiness	Overall, how would you describe your level of happiness? (1) Not at all happy (4) Very happy
Life satisfaction	Considering everything in your life, how satisfied are you with your life overall? (1) Completely dissatisfied (10) Completely satisfied
Trust in most people	In general, do you believe that most people can be trusted, or do you think you need to be cautious in dealing with others? (1) Most people can be trusted (2) Need to be very careful
Feeling secure in neighborhood	How secure do you currently feel in your neighborhood? (1) Very secure (4) Not secure at all
Trust in neighbors	How much do you trust the people in your neighborhood? (1) Completely trust (4) Do not trust at all
Trust in people known personally	How much do you trust people you know personally? (1) Completely trust (4) Do not trust at all
Trust in people met for the first time	How much do you trust people you meet for the first time? (1) Completely trust (4) Do not trust at all
Trust in family	How much do you trust your family? (1) Completely trust (2) Somewhat trust (3) Not very much (4) Do not trust at all
Feeling part of local community	To what extent do you feel like you are part of your local community? (1) Strongly agree (4) Strongly disagree
Importance of friends	How important are friends in your life? (1) Very important (4) Not at all important
Importance of family	How important is family in your life? (1) Very important (4) Not at all important
Membership in organizations	For each type of organization, indicate if you are an active member (1) or not a member (0): Charitable, Environmental Art/Music/ Education Religious, Sports/Recreation Professional Self-Help Group Labor Union Political Party
Importance of politics	How important is politics in your life? (1) Very important (4) Not at all important
Voting in local elections	In local elections, how often do you vote? (1) Always/usually (3) Never
Income	On a scale from 1 to 10, where 1 indicates the lowest income group and 10 indicates the highest income group, in which group is your household? (1) Lowest income group (10) Highest income group
Freedom of choice	How much freedom of choice and control do you feel you have in your life? (1) No choice at all (10) Complete freedom

"All things considered, how satisfied are you with your life as a whole these days?" The respondents were asked to rate their life satisfaction on a scale ranging from 1 to 10, with (1) being completely dissatisfied and (10) being completely satisfied. The responses concerning happiness were reversed from (1) not at all happy to (4) very happy.

On the basis of the literature, the factors that explain social capital can be categorized into three dimensions: trust, networks, and institutions. The trust is taken from how much the respondents trusted family, neighbors, most people in society, people know personally and people they meet for the first time, and they are secure in the neighborhood. Each variable was evaluated on a four-point Likert-type scale ranging from 1 to 4, in which a lower score indicates a higher level of trust. The variables related to trust that most people can evaluate are as follows: (1) Most people can be trusted, and (2) they need to be very careful.

Income is one of the most commonly analyzed economic factors, with results that point to a positive association with subjective well-being (Clark et al., 2006; Hagerty & Veenhoven, 2003). The information about the self-reported income scale in the dataset allows us to estimate measures of economic resources as determinants of subjective well-being.

The literature has shown that people with more freedom of choice are significantly more satisfied with their lives than others are (Abdur Rahman & Veenhoven, 2018; Growiec & Growiec, 2014). The variable freedom of choice was included in the model.

Networks were evaluated on the basis of respondents' engagement with organizations, the importance of family and friends, and civic participation. The model covered information on memberships in organizations, such as religious, sports, art and music, labor unions, political, professional, charitable/humanitarian organizations, and self-help groups. Membership in organizations was generalized as a dummy variable. The association membership variable takes a value of one/two if the respondent is a member of any of the 11 groups/associations listed in the survey and zero if they are not a member of any.

Table 5.11 presents the descriptive results of the variables. The average value of the variable of happiness was 3.61, and the standard deviation was 0.57. The average life satisfaction score was 7.9, with a standard deviation of 1.87. Among the respondents, 38.6% were engaged in any type of organization.

Descriptive statistics were used to present the fundamental information of the sample. Ordinary least squares regression models were developed to test the associations of income and freedom of choice as social capital variables with happiness and life satisfaction. These components of social capital—trust, networks, and institutions—were highlighted in the literature review and examined. The final table covers the overall impact on happiness and life satisfaction by combining all the determinants.

A one standard deviation increase in income scale is estimated to increase life satisfaction by approximately 0.30 standard deviations, while it is insignificant at the happiness level. The estimates' key aspect is that trust in most people, trust that people meet for the first time, and trust that people personally know lack statistical significance in both cases: happiness and life satisfaction. The models confirm the importance of social capital in interpreting trust in the family. The possibility of being a member of the local community and the importance of friends have strong explanatory power for the happiness and life satisfaction of Uzbek respondents.

Table 5.11 Variable description

Variable	Mean	Std. Dev	Min	Max
Happiness	3.61	0.57	1	4
Life satisfaction	7.90	1.87	1	10
Important in life: family	1.03	0.17	1	3
Important in life: friends	1.58	0.69	1	4
Freedom of choice	7.84	2.37	1	10
Income scale	5.83	1.78	1	10
Important in life: politics	2.57	1.00	1	4
Vote in a local election	1.44	0.63	1	3
Secure in neighborhood	1.48	0.79	1	4
Trust: people at the first meet	3.31	0.75	1	4
Trust: most people	1.86	0.35	1	2
Trust: neighborhood	1.69	0.77	1	4
Trust: family	1.03	0.21	1	4
Member of the local community	1.43	0.74	1	4
Trust: know people personally	1.99	0.91	1	4
Membership: religious organization	0.06	0.32	0	2
Membership: sport organization	0.05	0.29	0	2
Membership: art, music organization	0.18	0.50	0	2
Membership: labor unions	0.03	0.23	0	2
Membership: political party	0.04	0.24	0	2
Membership: environmental organization	0.04	0.24	0	2
Membership: professional organization	0.02	0.21	0	2
Membership: charitable/humanitarian organization	0.02	0.17	0	2
Membership: consumer organization	0.12	0.52	0	2
Membership: self-help groups	0.01	0.14	0	2
Membership: any other organization	0.02	0.18	0	2
Active membership	0.39	0.71	0	2
Number of observations	1283			

However, not all social capital variables are closely linked to subjective well-being. Notably, membership in sports, art and music organizations, political parties, charitable organizations, self-help groups, and any other organization has shown no significant relationship with subjective well-being, as shown in Table 5.3. Membership in religious and professional organizations and labor unions is significantly positively associated with happiness levels. Membership in religious and professional organizations may be voluntary, whereas labor unions are more related to public affairs (Table 5.12).

Table 5.12 Trust, network, and subjective well-being

	Happiness		Life satisfaction	
Freedom of choice	0.02*	0.014	0.10***	0.10***
Income scale	0.02	0.019	0.30***	0.31***
Secure in neighborhood	−0.09***		−0.08	
Trust: most people	−0.01		−0.09	
Trust: neighborhood	−0.04		−0.20*	
Trust: people know personally	−0.02		0.06	
Trust: people you meet for the first time	0.03		0.03	
Trust: family	−0.38***		−0.79**	
Member of my local community		−0.26***		
Important: family		−0.53***		−0.51
Important: friends		−0.15***		−0.19*
Membership: religious organization		0.12**		0.20
Membership: sport organization		−0.06		−0.07
Membership: art, music organization		−0.02		−0.13
Membership: labor unions		0.11*		0.25
Membership: political party		−0.14		0.29
Membership: professional organization		0.15*		0.02
Membership: charitable organization		0.07		−0.01
Membership: self-help groups		−0.14		−0.09
Membership: any other organization		−0.04		−0.29
_Cons	3.92***	4.31***	6.59***	6.52***
N	1283	1283	1283	1283
R^2	0.06	0.10	0.13	0.14

Legend *$p < 0.05$; **$p < 0.01$; ***$p < 0.001$

People who are actively engaged in local-level elections feel considerably happier. People who believe that politics is important in their lives are more satisfied than others are (see Table 5.4).

Table 5.4 examines subjective well-being and all social capital variables through OLS regression.

The results indicate that freedom of choice and income scale have statistically significant relationships with life satisfaction, with coefficients of 0.10 and 0.30, respectively. However, the coefficient for the income scale is statistically significant only for happiness at the 0.05 level. The most important variable associated with happiness is the importance of family, followed by trust in family and the importance of friends. On the other hand, the variable of life satisfaction is more associated with family trust, followed by the perceptions of members of the local community and voting in local-level elections. The results also indicate that being a member of the local community has a statistically significant relationship with life satisfaction, with

Table 5.13 Institutions, trust, networks, and subjective well-being

	Happiness		Life satisfaction	
Freedom of choice	0.02*	0.01	0.10***	0.10***
Income scale	0.02	0.02	0.30***	0.30***
Political participation				
Important: politics	−0.03	−0.01	−0.17**	−0.14**
Vote in elections: local level	−0.08**	−0.02	0.06	0.18*
Secure In neighborhood		−0.08***		−0.09
Trust: most people		−0.01		−0.06
Trust: neighborhood		−0.00		−0.16*
Trust: people know personally		−0.01		0.06
Trust: people you meet for the first time		0.03		0.04
Trust: family		−0.31**		−0.73**
Member of my local community		−0.09***		−0.28***
Important: family		−0.44***		−0.35
Important: friends		−0.14***		-0.14
Active membership		0.01		0.03
_cons	3.54***	4.67***	5.67***	7.48***
N	1283	1283	1283	1283
R^2	0.02	0.12	0.12	0.16

Legend *$p < 0.05$; **$p < 0.01$; ***$p < 0.001$

a coefficient of −0.28. The variables related to political participation, such as the importance of politics and voting in local elections, also have statistically significant relationships with life satisfaction, with coefficients of −0.17 (−0.14) and 0.18, respectively (Table 5.13).

All control variables associated with life satisfaction are statistically significant, although the model with happiness results in no significant association with freedom of choice or the income scale.

5.6 Discussion

In this research, I analyzed data collected from the World Values Survey and examined the relationship between social capital and subjective well-being. I presented a cross-sectional association between social capital and happiness and life satisfaction, adjusting for the scale of income and freedom of choice.

The existing research has consistently highlighted the significance of trust and social capital to subjective well-being (Bjørnskov, 2008; Brehm & Rahn, 1997). In this regard, the study revealed that trust in the family was an essential predictor of happiness and life satisfaction in Uzbekistan. This result indicates that trust in the family seems to be quite significant in explaining social capital and represents an essential component in the link between trust and subjective well-being in Uzbekistan. Our results contrast with the positive externalities on trusting and trust-neutral people, who answer that they can trust others/most people (Kuroki, 2011). The results on trust in most people and people who know personally show that both happiness and life satisfaction are not statistically significant.

Additionally, the literature emphasizes the impact of neighborhood security on happiness, indicating that individuals with high levels of happiness are more likely to reside in safe, low-crime areas. This aligns with broader research on the influence of neighborhood factors on subjective well-being, emphasizing the interplay between physical safety and well-being (Cheng & Smyth, 2015).

Social networks also play a significant role in connecting people, which can contribute to the well-being of individuals. By enabling individuals to form meaningful relationships and engage with like-minded individuals, social networks foster a sense of community and belonging that is essential to happiness in Uzbekistan. Interestingly, research has shown that social connections have a greater impact on one's life satisfaction than does income or freedom of choice. This holds particularly true for Uzbek society, which has been considered a collectivist culture. In such cultures, social networks play a critical role in shaping an individual's identity, beliefs, and behaviors. Therefore, it is essential to have strong social connections and maintain healthy relationships with family and friends for a fulfilling and happy life. As Bjornskov's study illustrated that membership in associations is weakly related to trust, our results related to membership in voluntary organizations have no statistically significant impact on either happiness or life satisfaction in Uzbekistan (Bjørnskov, 2006).

Overall, the research emphasized the importance of social capital in enhancing well-being. This highlights how having a strong network of social connections, trust, and mutual support can positively impact our lives.

Over the past few years, interest in investigating subjective well-being has increased. While economic factors have been studied extensively, there is still a need for more research on how noneconomic factors such as social capital can impact subjective well-being. The level of social capital within a country can be a strong indicator of the overall sense of well-being among its citizens. However, in regard to the impact of economic growth on this relationship, the research has been inconclusive, with varying results depending on the country. One notable exception to this is in transition countries, where there is a general consensus that economic growth has a significant effect on well-being. This raises the question of whether social capital has a weaker effect in these countries because of the greater emphasis on financial wealth as a source of happiness. Essentially, this asks whether the relationship between social capital and well-being is less reliable in transition countries than in other nations. This study examines how social capital and its components impact subjective well-being in Uzbekistan via data from the World Values Survey. The study shows that social networks, trust, and political participation/institutions have varying impacts on happiness and life satisfaction. While social networks and trust positively affect happiness, trust in institutions does not. However, they remain important for life satisfaction.

The implications of this study's findings for policymakers and researchers interested in improving subjective well-being in Uzbekistan could include the need to focus on fostering trust, promoting participation in social activities, and emphasizing the importance of politics. Additionally, the study's emphasis on the impact of trust in family and local community membership on subjective well-being suggests that policymakers could consider initiatives aimed at strengthening social connections and community engagement.

It is essential to acknowledge the research limitations of this paper for future studies. The analysis in this paper uses cross-sectional data, which makes it impossible to determine the causal relationship between happiness and social capital measurement. Therefore, the use of longitudinal data is recommended in future research to obtain more precise results.

In conclusion, the social norms in Central Asia, deeply rooted in traditions and cultural practices, play a significant role in shaping perceptions of happiness and subjective well-being in the region. These norms, influenced by collectivist values and traditional family structures, impact various aspects of life, including family dynamics, gender roles, and community engagement. While these social norms contribute to networks of support and mutual aid, they can also enforce conformity and limit personal autonomy, affecting individual satisfaction differently. Additionally, the complex interplay between social norms and happiness emphasizes the importance of cultural context in shaping well-being. Furthermore, the construction of a new national identity in Kazakhstan after gaining independence has been influenced by the Soviet legacy, government initiatives, and societal reactions. The historical context of Soviet intervention and the demographic mix of the population have contributed to the complexities of forging a unified national identity. The government's efforts to promote Kazakh culture and language while preserving multiculturalism have been significant in shaping the post-independence identity. Understanding the influence of social norms and national identity on happiness and well-being in Central Asia is essential for addressing the broader implications of these factors on individual and collective life satisfaction. It is crucial to continue exploring these dynamics through both empirical studies and theoretical perspectives to develop a comprehensive understanding of how these norms collectively impact subjective well-being in the region.

5.7 Conclusion

A comparative analysis of subjective well-being (SWB) determinants in Central Asia against established Western literature reveals both important convergences and instructive divergences that challenge universal assumptions about happiness. The strong positive association between freedom of choice and SWB ($\beta = 0.27$–0.51) in Kazakhstan and Kyrgyzstan data aligns with Western self-determination theory

(Ryan & Deci, 2000), yet manifests differently in practice due to distinct political contexts. While Western studies emphasize institutional trust in democratic systems (Helliwell & Huang, 2008), Central Asia demonstrates that perceived freedom retains predictive power even in more authoritarian settings, suggesting the cross-cultural validity of autonomy needs but varying pathways to their fulfillment. The finding that marriage shows weaker positive effects than divorce reveals negative impacts (−0.61*** in Kazakhstan), partially supporting Western marital advantage theories (Waite & Gallagher, 2001), while also highlighting culturally specific family dynamics in which marital dissolution may carry a greater social stigma in collectivist societies. Tajik data shows single individuals reporting higher life satisfaction than married counterparts (β = 1.42* vs. 0.58*), directly opposing the well-established marital advantage theory (Waite & Gallagher, 2001). This may reflect the economic burdens of traditional wedding customs (e.g., "qalin" bride price) or differing family expectations. Uzbekistan displays more conventional patterns, with married individuals showing higher happiness (β = 0.39***), suggesting intra-regional cultural variations in family dynamics.

In Tajikistan, financial satisfaction emerges as the strongest predictor of life satisfaction (β = 0.52*, $p < 0.001$), exceeding effect sizes typically observed in Western studies. This aligns with Maslow's hierarchy in developing economies, where basic needs fulfillment remains paramount. Conversely, Uzbekistan presents a counterintuitive negative association between financial satisfaction and happiness (β = −0.05*), suggesting either measurement artifacts or a unique cultural valuation of non-material well-being. Health status shows robust negative coefficients in Uzbekistan (β = −0.39*** for life satisfaction), nearly triple the effect size found in European samples, highlighting the acute well-being consequences of healthcare deficiencies.

The most striking departure from Western literature is evident in gender effects, where Central Asian data reveal no significant differences, in contrast to the robust findings of gender gaps in Western studies (Stevenson & Wolfers, 2009). This challenges biological explanations of gender differences in SWB and suggests cultural mediation, possibly through more prescribed (but equally valued) social roles in traditional societies. Similarly, education's inconsistent effects—including negative coefficients in Kyrgyzstan (β = −0.10*)—contradict the nearly universal positive education-SWB correlation found in Western research, potentially reflecting post-Soviet labor market distortions where educational attainment doesn't guarantee status or income mobility.

The counterintuitive positive association between unemployment and happiness in Kyrgyzstan (β = 0.12*) directly contradicts Western findings (Paul & Moser, 2009) but may align with emerging research on informal economies (Williams & Horodnic, 2017) and communal coping mechanisms in developing contexts. This suggests unemployment may carry different psychological meanings in societies with weaker formal labor market attachments. The significant effect of political satisfaction (β = 0.17***) mirrors Western findings about governance quality (Frey & Stutzer, 2002) but operates through different mechanisms in hybrid regimes, where basic political stability may outweigh democratic participation concerns. Tajikistan demonstrates no significant employment effects, whereas Uzbekistan exhibits negative coefficients for employed status across multiple indicators. This pattern may be attributed to several factors, including the pervasive presence of informal economies that diminish the psychological impact of formal employment, lingering distortions in the labor market stemming from the Soviet era, and the existence of alternative value systems in which work is not central to personal identity. Furthermore, education consistently shows non-significant or even negative effects on outcomes in both countries, a finding that stands in stark contrast to Western human capital models, where education is typically associated with positive labor market returns.

The analysis indicates that political factors such as confidence in government, democratic system satisfaction, and political engagement exhibit mixed associations with SWB. For instance, in Kazakhstan, confidence in government was negatively associated with life satisfaction and happiness in Wave 7, while satisfaction with the democratic system had a positive association in Wave 6. These findings partially align with Western literature, where trust in institutions and democratic governance is generally linked to higher SWB (Helliwell & Huang, 2008). However, the negative association between confidence in government and SWB in Kazakhstan suggests a potential divergence, possibly due to political disillusionment or governance challenges unique to the region.

In Kyrgyzstan, the importance of democracy was positively linked to life satisfaction (Wave 6), whereas interest in politics was negatively associated with it. This contrasts with Western studies, where political engagement often correlates with higher SWB (Frey & Stutzer, 2000). The discrepancy may stem from differing political climates, where political participation in less stable democracies may induce stress rather than fulfillment.

In Tajikistan, satisfaction with politics and perceived freedom of choice were strongly associated with higher life satisfaction ($\beta = 0.17^{***}$ and $\beta = 0.30^{***}$, respectively), suggesting that political autonomy and effective governance play a meaningful role in well-being. This aligns partially with Western literature, where political efficacy is linked to greater life satisfaction. However, unlike in stable democracies, interest in politics had no significant effect—possibly due to limited avenues for meaningful civic engagement. Economic factors like income and health were also key predictors, reinforcing the interplay between material security and SWB.

In contrast, Uzbekistan exhibited a stark negative relationship between confidence in government and life satisfaction ($\beta = -0.68^{*}$), one of the strongest effects observed in the region. This may reflect deep-seated distrust in authoritarian governance, where state institutions are perceived as ineffective or oppressive. Unlike Tajikistan, political factors such as democratic values or electoral participation showed minimal impact on SWB, possibly due to suppressed political freedoms reducing expectations. Instead, economic stability (income scale: $\beta = 0.26^{*}$) and marital status (divorce sharply reduced happiness: $\beta = -0.56^{***}$) were more salient, highlighting the primacy of personal and financial security over political engagement.

In Kazakhstan, valuing family was positively associated with life satisfaction (Wave 6: $\beta = 0.21$), whereas in Kyrgyzstan, it showed no significant effect. This contrasts with Western studies, where family cohesion is consistently linked to higher SWB (Diener et al., 2018). The negative association between "importance of friends" and SWB in Kazakhstan (Wave 7: $\beta = -0.37^{***}$) further deviates from Western norms, possibly reflecting cultural differences in social trust dynamics.

In Kyrgyzstan, pride in nationality was negatively associated with happiness (Wave 6: $\beta = -0.11^{***}$), a surprising result given that national pride typically enhances SWB in collectivist societies. This may indicate political disillusionment or economic frustrations outweighing patriotic sentiment.

While "importance of family" was positively associated with life satisfaction ($\beta = 0.27$), being married had a weaker effect on happiness ($\beta = 0.30^{*}$) compared to Western studies where marriage typically shows stronger benefits.

Surprisingly, valuing work was negatively associated with both life satisfaction ($\beta = -0.20^{*}$) and happiness ($\beta = -0.06^{*}$), contradicting Western findings where work centrality enhances SWB (Steptoe et al., 2003). This may reflect labor market frustrations in Tajikistan's struggling economy.

The belief that "women's income is problematic" was positively linked to life satisfaction ($\beta = 0.19^{***}$), suggesting traditional gender roles may provide stability in this context. Membership in religious organizations increased happiness ($\beta = 0.12^{**}$), aligning with global patterns of religiosity's psychological benefits (Lim & Putnam, 2010). "Freedom of choice" showed stronger effects in Uzbekistan ($\beta = 0.10^{***}$) than typically found in Western studies, possibly because basic autonomy matters more in restrictive environments.

To advance the understanding of SWB in Central Asia, researchers are encouraged to employ mixed-methods designs that integrate both quantitative and qualitative methodologies. While quantitative surveys can provide broad, generalizable insights into patterns of well-being, qualitative interviews and focus groups are indispensable for uncovering the nuanced ways in which political perceptions, cultural norms, and historical legacies shape subjective experiences of well-being. The integration of qualitative data can illuminate context-specific determinants of SWB that may be overlooked by standardized survey instruments.

Future research on subjective well-being in Central Asia should take several steps. Firstly, comparative studies encompassing Uzbekistan, Tajikistan, and Turkmenistan are warranted to assess whether and how different political systems—ranging from authoritarian to semi-democratic regimes—differentially impact SWB. Existing literature suggests that political stability, the rule of law, and the degree of personal and media freedoms are significant predictors of well-being in the region. Secondly, longitudinal research designs are essential for capturing the dynamic relationship between political change (e.g., mass protests, leadership transitions) and trajectories of subjective well-being over time. Thirdly, subnational analyses comparing urban and rural populations are crucial. Urban and rural residents may differ markedly in their exposure to political processes, economic opportunities, and social support networks, all of which are established determinants of SWB. Additionally, future research should also consider the interplay between cultural values and political systems. For example, the extent to which local leadership discourses align modern political systems with traditional cultural values may influence public perceptions of legitimacy and, by extension, well-being.

By implementing the following recommendations, policymakers can create more effective strategies to enhance subjective well-being in Central Asia, aligning with the distinct cultural and socioeconomic factors at play while challenging universal assumptions about happiness.

- Enhance policies that foster individual freedom and choice, even within more authoritarian contexts. Recognizing the strong link between perceived freedom and subjective well-being can guide the development of programs that empower citizens, allowing them to make decisions that impact their lives positively.
- Given the varied impacts of marital status on happiness across Central Asian countries, policymakers should consider the sociocultural contexts surrounding marriage. Support systems for single individuals, along with resources that alleviate the economic burden of traditional marriage customs, could enhance overall well-being.
- Develop economic policies that prioritize financial stability and job creation, particularly in Tajikistan, where financial satisfaction is crucial for life satisfaction. Initiatives should focus on improving economic opportunities and providing access to financial education to help citizens manage their finances better.
- Given the significant negative impact of health status on well-being in Central Asia, policymakers must prioritize healthcare improvements. Increasing access to quality healthcare services can mitigate the acute consequences of healthcare deficiencies on subjective well-being.
- Since gender differences in subjective well-being appear less pronounced in Central Asia than in Western studies, policies should be tailored to address cultural contexts rather than universal assumptions. Initiatives promoting gender equality and addressing prescribed social roles may improve subjective well-being for all genders.
- With inconsistent effects of education on well-being in the region, revising educational programs to align more closely with labor market needs is vital. Focus on vocational training and skills development that can directly enhance employment prospects and economic mobility.
- Given the positive association between unemployment and happiness in Kyrgyzstan, consider ways to integrate informal economies into formal frameworks. Support for informal job sectors and communal coping strategies can harness strengths in these networks while ensuring economic sustainability.
- Strengthening confidence in governmental institutions and improving democratic engagement is essential. Policymakers should work to foster transparency and responsiveness in governance, which can contribute to higher levels of subjective well-being, as evidenced in mixed associations with political satisfaction.
- Recognize the unique cultural context of work and employment in Central Asia. Policies should promote employment that aligns with the community's values and social structures, while also considering the psychological effects of informal employment and societal attitudes toward work.

- Initiate longitudinal studies on well-being determinants in Central Asia to continue identifying region-specific trends. Policymakers should utilize this research to inform evidence-based policymaking that reflects the unique socioeconomic and cultural landscapes of the region.

References

Abdur Rahman, A., & Veenhoven, R. (2018). Freedom and Happiness in Nations: A Research Synthesis. *Applied Research in Quality of Life, 13*(2), 435–456.

"Analytical tables - Agency on statistics under the President of the Republic of Tajikistan." (2023). *Агентии омори назди Президенти Ҷумҳурии Тоҷикистон* (blog). https://www.stat.tj/en/analytical-tables/

Alkire, S. (2005). Subjective Quantitative Studies of Human Agency. *Social Indicators Research, 74*(1), 217–260. https://doi.org/10.1007/s11205-005-6525-0

Anand, P., Hunter, G., & Smith, R. (2005). Capabilities and Well-Being: Evidence Based on the Sen-Nussbaum Approach to Welfare. *Social Indicators Research, 74*(1), 9–55. https://doi.org/10.1007/s11205-005-6518-z

Bartolini, S., Mikucka, M., & Sarracino, F. (2017). Money, Trust and Happiness in Transition Countries: Evidence from Time Series. *Social Indicators Research, 130*(1), 87–106. https://doi.org/10.1007/s11205-015-1130-3

Batsaikhan, U., & Dabrowski, M. (2017). Central Asia—Twenty-Five Years After the Breakup of the USSR. *Russian Journal of Economics, 3*(3), 296–320.

Bhuiyan, S. (2012). Political Leadership and Its Role in Achieving Good Governance in Kazakhstan. *International Journal of Public Administration, 35*(6), 379–388. https://doi.org/10.1080/01900692.2012.655525

Bian, Y., Hao, M., & Li, Y. (2018). Social Networks and Subjective Well-Being: A Comparison of Australia, Britain, and China. *Journal of Happiness Studies, 19*(8), 2489–2508. https://doi.org/10.1007/s10902-017-9926-2

Bjørnskov, C. (2003). The Happy Few: Cross-Country Evidence on Social Capital and Life Satisfaction. Available at SSRN 381640.

Bjørnskov, C. (2006). The Multiple Facets of Social Capital. *European Journal of Political Economy, 22*(1), 22–40.

Bjørnskov, C. (2008). Social Capital and Happiness in the United States. *Applied Research in Quality of Life, 3*, 43–62.

Blackburn, M. (2019). Discourses of Russian-Speaking Youth in Nazarbayev's Kazakhstan: Soviet Legacies and Responses to Nation-Building. *Central Asian Survey, 38*(2), 217–236.

Blanchflower, D. G., & Oswald, A. J. (2008). Is Well-Being U-Shaped over the Life Cycle? *Social Science & Medicine, 66*(8), 1733–1749.

Borisova, E. (2024). *Paradoxes of Migration in Tajikistan: Locating the Good Life*. UCL Press. https://books.google.com/books?hl=en&lr=&id=S68FEQAAQBAJ&oi=fnd&pg=PP1&dq=Economic+factors+of+happiness+in+Tajikistan&ots=ptgWwZsRdp&sig=0EInHqxKn1pBlMJx71eLNZM1uZU

Brehm, J., & Rahn, W. 1997. Individual-Level Evidence for the Causes and Consequences of Social Capital. *American Journal of Political Science*, 999–1023.

Burkhanov, A. 2017. Kazakhstan's National Identity—Building Policy: Soviet Legacy, State Efforts, and Societal Reactions. *Cornell International Law Journal, 50*, 1. https://heinonline.org/HOL/LandingPage?handle=hein.journals/cintl50&div=4&id=&page=

Burkhanov, A. (2018). Policy-making styles in Central Asia: The Soviet legacy and new institutions. In Policy Styles and Policy-Making (pp. 222–241). Routledge.

Cheng, Z., & Smyth, R. (2015). Crime Victimization, Neighborhood Safety and Happiness in China. *Economic Modelling, 51*, 424–435.

Clark, A. E., Frijters, P., & Shields, M. A. (2006). *Income and Happiness: Evidence, Explanations and Economic Implications*. https://shs.hal.science/halshs-00590436/

Clark, A. E., Flèche, S., Layard, R., & Powdthavee, N., & Ward, G. (2017). *The Key Determinants of Happiness and Misery*. https://eprints.lse.ac.uk/83622

Collins, K., & Gambrel, R. (2017). Corruption and Popular Support for Democracy and Government in Transitional Contexts: The Case of Kyrgyzstan. *Europe-Asia Studies, 69*(8), 1280–1309. https://doi.org/10.1080/09668136.2017.1384449

Cummings, S. N., & Ryabkov, M. (2013). Situating the 'Tulip Revolution.' In *Domestic and International Perspectives on Kyrgyzstan's 'Tulip Revolution'* (pp. 19–30). Routledge. https://doi.org/10.4324/9781315876092-4&type=chapterpdf.

Dadabaev, T. (2007). Trajectories of Political Development and Public Choices in Turkmenistan. *Asian Affairs: An American Review, 34*(3), 131–150. https://doi.org/10.3200/AAFS.34.3.131-150

Deci, E. L., & Ryan, R. M. (2012). Self-Determination Theory. *Handbook of Theories of Social Psychology, 1*(20), 416–436.

Delhey, J., Hess, S., Boehnke, K., Deutsch, F., Eichhorn, J., Kühnen, U., & Welzel, C. (2023). Life Satisfaction during the COVID-19 Pandemic: The Role of Human, Economic, Social, and Psychological Capital. *Journal of Happiness Studies, 24*(7), 2201–2222.

Demircioglu, M. A., & Sharipova, D. (2023). Does Public Sector Employment Matter for Subjective Well-Being? The Case of Kazakhstan. *International Journal of Public Administration*, 1–16.

"Demografiya." 2024. (2024). https://stat.uz/uz/rasmiy-statistika/demography-2

Diener, A. C. (2005). Kazakhstan's Kin State Diaspora: Settlement Planning and the Oralman Dilemma. *Europe-Asia Studies, 57*(2), 327–348. https://doi.org/10.1080/09668130500052005

Diener, E. (2000). Subjective Well-Being: The Science of Happiness and a Proposal for a National Index. *American Psychologist,* 55(1), 34.

Diener, E., & Biswas-Diener, R. (2002). [No Title Found]. *Social Indicators Research, 57*(2), 119–169. https://doi.org/10.1023/A:1014411319119

Diener, E., & Chan, M. Y. (2011). Happy People Live Longer: Subjective Well-Being Contributes to Health and Longevity: HEALTH BENEFITS OF HAPPINESS. *Applied Psychology: Health and Well-Being, 3*(1), 1–43. https://doi.org/10.1111/j.1758-0854.2010.01045.x.

Diener, E., & Seligman, M. E. P. (2004). Beyond Money: Toward an Economy of Well-Being. *Psychological Science in the Public Interest,* 5(1), 1–31. https://doi.org/10.1111/j.0963-7214.2004.00501001.x

Diener, E., Suh, E. M., Lucas, R. E., & Smith, H. L. (1999). Subjective Well-Being: Three Decades of Progress. *Psychological Bulletin, 125*(2), 276.

Diener, E., Diener, C., Choi, H., & Oishi, S. (2018). Revisiting 'Most People Are Happy'—And Discovering When They Are Not. *Perspectives on Psychological Science, 13*(2), 166–170. https://doi.org/10.1177/1745691618765111

Dolan, P., & Peasgood, T. (2008). Measuring Well-Being for Public Policy: Preferences or Experiences? *The Journal of Legal Studies, 37*(S2), S5-31. https://doi.org/10.1086/595676

Easterlin, R. A. (2001). Income and Happiness: Towards a Unified Theory. *The Economic Journal, 111*(473), 465–484. https://doi.org/10.1111/1468-0297.00646

Ekici, T., & Koydemir, S. (2014). Social Capital, Government and Democracy Satisfaction, and Happiness in Turkey: A Comparison of Surveys in 1999 and 2008. *Social Indicators Research, 118*, 1031–1053.

Falkingham, J. (2000). *Women and Gender Relations in Tajikistan.* Asian Development Bank, Programs Department East and Office of Environment …. https://www.adb.org/sites/default/files/institutional-document/32601/women-tajikistan.pdf

Flavin, P., & Keane, M. J. (2012). Life Satisfaction and Political Participation: Evidence from the United States. *Journal of Happiness Studies, 13*(1), 63–78. https://doi.org/10.1007/s10902-011-9250-1

Frey, B. S., & Stutzer, A. (2000). Happiness, economy and institutions. *The Economic Journal, 110*(466), 918–938.

Frey, B. S., & Stutzer, A. (2002). What can economists learn from happiness research?. *Journal of Economic Literature, 40*(2), 402–435.

Gauntlett, D. (2018). *Making Is Connecting: The Social Power of Creativity, from Craft and Knitting to Digital Everything.* Wiley. https://books.google.com/books?hl=en&lr=&id=VpNcDwAAQBAJ&oi=fnd&pg=PT7&dq=David+Gauntlett,+Making+Is+Connecting:+The+Social+Power+of+Creativity,+from+Craft+and+Knitting+to+Digital+Everything+(John+Wiley+%26+Sons,+2018),+&ots=3Mx4MbWysD&sig=9AfqvnDp_0FrDa5tRY9LWtUrKa8

Graham, C. (2008). Happiness and Health: Lessons—And Questions—For Public Policy. *Health Affairs, 27*(1), 72–87. https://doi.org/10.1377/hlthaff.27.1.72

Growiec, K., & Growiec, J. (2014). Trusting Only Whom You Know, Knowing Only Whom You Trust: The Joint Impact of Social Capital and Trust on Happiness in CEE Countries. *Journal of Happiness Studies, 15*(5), 1015–1040. https://doi.org/10.1007/s10902-013-9461-8

Gullette, D. (2010). Institutionalized Instability: Factors Leading to the April 2010 Uprising in Kyrgyzstan. *Eurasian Review, 3*, 89–105.

Guriev, S., & Melnikov, N. (2018). Happiness Convergence in Transition Countries. *Journal of Comparative Economics, 46*(3), 683–707.

Haerpfer, C., Inglehart, R., Moreno, A., Welzel, C., Kizilova, K., Diez-Medrano J., M. Lagos, P. Norris, E. Ponarin & B. Puranen et al. (eds.). 2020. World Values Survey: Round Seven—Country-Pooled Datafile. Madrid, Spain & Vienna, Austria: JD Systems Institute & WVSA Secretariat. https://doi.org/10.14281/18241.1

Hagerty, M. R., & Veenhoven, R. (2003). Wealth and Happiness Revisited-Growing National Income Does Go with Greater Happiness. *Social Indicators Research, 64*, 1–27.

Harris, C. (2000). The Changing Identity of Women in Tajikistan in the Post-Soviet Period. In *Gender and Identity Construction: Women of Central Asia, the Caucasus, and Turkey, Edited by Feride Acar and Ayse G.* https://brill.com/downloadpdf/display/book/edcoll/9789004492028/B9789004492028_s013.pdf

Helliwell, J. F., & Putnam, R. D. (2004). The Social Context of Well–Being. In F. A. Huppert, N. Baylis, & B. Keverne (Eds.), *Philosophical Transactions of the Royal Society of London. Series B: Biological Sciences, 359*(1449), 1435–1446. https://doi.org/10.1098/rstb.2004.1522

Helliwell, J. F., & Huang, H. (2008). How's Your Government? International Evidence Linking Good Government and Well-Being. *British Journal of Political Science, 38*(4), 595–619.

Hofstede, G. (2001). *Culture's Consequences: Comparing Values, Behaviors, Institutions and Organizations across Nations.* Sage publications. https://books.google.com/books?hl=en&lr=&id=9HE-DQAAQBAJ&oi=fnd&pg=PP1&dq=Hofstede,+2001&ots=lMv8sRy2SV&sig=ily-H197XfSVeSprBuqDUidd9gU

Hommerich, C., & Tiefenbach, T. (2018). Analyzing the Relationship between Social Capital and Subjective Well-Being: The Mediating Role of Social Affiliation. *Journal of Happiness Studies, 19*, 1091–1114.

Inglehart, R. (1997). Modernization, Postmodernization and Changing Perceptions of Risk. *International Review of Sociology, 7*(3), 449–459. https://doi.org/10.1080/03906701.1997.9971250

Inglehart, R. (2020). *Modernization and Postmodernization: Cultural, Economic, and Political Change in 43 Societies.* Princeton University Press. https://books.google.com/books?hl=en&lr=&id=D9PgDwAAQBAJ&oi=fnd&pg=PA3&dq=Modernization+and+Postmodernization:+Cultural,+Economic,+and+Political+Change+in+43+Societies&ots=OKDoIRQler&sig=LLBf1E6othLO23tVttaQMIilfCU

Ifert Johnson, D. (2006). Music Videos and National Identity in Post-Soviet Kazakhstan. *Qualitative Research Reports in Communication, 7*(1), 9–14. https://doi.org/10.1080/17459430600964513.

"Infant Mortality." 2024. 2024. https://bala.stat.gov.kz/en/mladencheskaya-smertnost/.

Inoguchi, T., & Fujii, S. (2012). *The Quality of Life in Asia: A Comparison of Quality of Life in Asia.* Springer Science & Business Media.

Inglehart, R., C. Haerpfer, A. Moreno, C. Welzel, K. Kizilova, J. Diez-Medrano, M. Lagos, P. Norris, E. Ponarin & B. Puranen et al. (eds.). (2018a). *World Values Survey: Round Six - Country Pooled Datafile*. Madrid, Spain & Vienna, Austria: JD Systems Institute & WVSA Secretariat. https://doi.org/10.14281/18241.8

Inglehart, R., C. Haerpfer, A. Moreno, C. Welzel, K. Kizilova, J. Diez-Medrano, M. Lagos, P. Norris, E. Ponarin & B. Puranen et al. (eds.). (2018b). *World Values Survey: Round Four - Country Pooled Datafile*. Madrid, Spain & Vienna, Austria: JD Systems Institute & WVSA Secretariat. https://doi.org/10.14281/18241.6

Kalmijn, M. (2005). The Effects of Divorce on Men's Employment and Social Security Histories. *European Journal of Population/Revue Européenne de Démographie, 21*(4), 347–366. https://doi.org/10.1007/s10680-005-0200-7

Kalyuzhnova, Y., & Patterson, K. (2016). Kazakhstan: Long-Term Economic Growth and the Role of the Oil Sector. *Comparative Economic Studies, 58*(1), 93–118. https://doi.org/10.1057/ces.2015.31

Kamp, M. (2009). Women's Studies and Gender Studies in Central Asia: Are We Talking to One Another. *Central Eurasian Studies Review, 8*(1), 2–12.

Kamp, M., & Nurdinova, S. (2022). Uzbek Migrants in Türkiye. *Region, 11*(2), 193–210.

Kesici, O. (2011). The Dilemma in the Nation-Building Process: The Kazakh or Kazakhstani Nation. *Journal on Ethnopolitics and Minority Issues in Europe, 10*, 31. https://heinonline.org/HOL/LandingPage?handle=hein.journals/jemie2011&div=4&id=&page=

Kim, S. (2023). Comparison of Happiness Levels in Central Asian Countries. *Journal of the Korea Society of Computer and Information, 28*(6), 145–152.

Kudebayeva, A., Sharipova, A., & Sharipova, D. (2022). Social Capital and Subjective Well-Being in Central Asia. *Europe-Asia Studies, 74*(1), 101–124. https://doi.org/10.1080/09668136.2021.1973965

Kuroki, M. (2011). "DOES SOCIAL TRUST INCREASE INDIVIDUAL HAPPINESS IN JAPAN?*: M. Kuroki: Happiness and Trust." *Japanese Economic Review, 62*(4), 444–459. https://doi.org/10.1111/j.1468-5876.2011.00533.x

Kuşçu, I. (2013). Ethnic Return Migration and Public Debate: The Case of Kazakhstan. *International Migration, 52*(2), 178–197. https://doi.org/10.1111/imig.12055

Laruelle, M., Huchet, J.-F., Peyrouse, S., & Balci, B. (2010). Why Central Asia? The Strategic Rationale of Indian and Chinese Involvement in the Region. In M. Laruelle, J.-F. Huchet, S. Peyrouse, & B. Balci (Eds.), *China and India in Central Asia* (pp. 1–6). Palgrave Macmillan US. https://doi.org/10.1057/9780230114357_1

Li, J., Chen, Y., Li, Z., & Huang, X. (2019). Low-Carbon Economic Development in Central Asia Based on LMDI Decomposition and Comparative Decoupling Analyses. *Journal of Arid Land, 11*(4), 513–524. https://doi.org/10.1007/s40333-019-0063-0

"Life Expectancy at Birth of the Population of the Republic of Kazakhstan (2023)." (2023). https://stat.gov.kz/en/industries/social-statistics/demography/publications/157663/.

Lim, C., & Putnam, R. D. (2010). Religion, social networks, and life satisfaction. *American Sociological Review, 75*(6), 914–933.

Lu, H., Tong, P., & Zhu, R. (2020). Longitudinal Evidence on Social Trust and Happiness in China: Causal Effects and Mechanisms. *Journal of Happiness Studies, 21*, 1841–1858.

Luhmann, M., Hofmann, W., Eid, M., & Lucas, R. E. (2012). Subjective Well-Being and Adaptation to Life Events: A Meta-Analysis. *Journal of Personality and Social Psychology, 102*(3), 592.

Makulbayeva, G. A., Davletbayeva, Z. Z., & Dyussenov, M. M. (2023). Subjective Well-Being in Central Asia: Rural-Urban Differences, *145*(4), 363–373.

Marat, E. (2006). *The Tulip Revolution: Kyrgyzstan One Year After*. Jamestown Foundation Washington, DC. https://www.academia.edu/download/12961445/The_Tulip_Revolution.pdf

Marmot, M., & Bobak, M. (2005). Social and Economic Changes and Health in Europe East and West. *European Review, 13*(1), 15–31.

Matsushima, M., & Matsunaga, Y. (2015). Social Capital and Subjective Well-Being in Japan. *VOLUNTAS: International Journal of Voluntary and Nonprofit Organizations, 26*, 1016–1045.

McKee-Ryan, F., Song, Z., Wanberg, C. R., & Kinicki, A. J. (2005). Psychological and Physical Well-Being during Unemployment: A Meta-Analytic Study. *Journal of Applied Psychology, 90*(1), 53.

Meeks, R. (2012). *Culture and Gender Roles: Evidence from a Natural Experiment in Post-Soviet Central Asia.* https://www.dartmouth.edu/neudc2012/docs/paper_258.pdf

Megoran, N. (2010). The Uzbekistan-Kyrgyzstan Boundary: Stalin's Cartography, Post-Soviet Geography. In *Borderliness and Borderlands: Political Oddities at the Edge of the Nation-State* (pp. 33–52).

"Migration and Development Brief 38 | KNOMAD." (2023). https://knomad.org/publication/migration-and-development-brief-38

Myers, D. G. (2000). The Funds, Friends, and Faith of Happy People. *American Psychologist, 55*(1), 56.

Naghdi, Y., Amirtaemeh, H., & Kaghazian, S. (2021). The Puzzle of Relationship between the Economic Growth and Happiness. *Economic Analysis, 54*(1), 1–12.

Neira Gómez, I., Lacalle-Calderon, M., Portela, M., & Trujillo, M. P. n.d. Social Capital Dimensions and Subjective Wellbeing: A Quantile Approach. https://minerva.usc.es/xmlui/handle/10347/32144. Accessed April 16, 2024.

Omarova, A., & Kenzhakimov, G. (2023). Sociological Measurement of the Happiness Index in Central Asian Countries. *Journal of Community Positive Practices, 1*, 17–28.

Oreopoulos, P. (2008). Priceless: The Nonpecuniary Benefits of Schooling. *Journal of Economic Perspectives, 25*(1), 1516.

Osmonova, D., Talgarbekova, E., Tashtanbekova, M., Moldoshova, A., & Anastassiadi, A. (2023). Evolution of Family Relationship in Kyrgyzstan. *Social and Legal Studios, 6*(4), 155–163.

Özkan, A., Kamalova, B. F., Baitenova, N. Z., & Kantarbaeva, Z. (2019). The Effect of Sacred Sited in Kazakhstan on Society Their Place in the Conservation of National Identity. *Journal for the Study of Religions and Ideologies, 18*, 203–217. https://www.jsri.ro/ojs/index.php/jsri/article/download/1147/829.

Paul, K. I., & Moser, K. (2009). Unemployment impairs mental health: Meta-analyses. *Journal of Vocational Behavior, 74*(3), 264–282.

Peyrouse, S. (2007). Nationhood and the Minority Question in Central Asia. The Russians in Kazakhstan. *Europe-Asia Studies, 59*(3), 481–501. https://doi.org/10.1080/09668130701239930

"Population - Official Statistics - Statistics of the Kyrgyz Republic." (2024). https://stat.gov.kg/en/statistics/naselenie/

"Population of the Republic of Kazakhstan by Gender and Type of Locality (as of April 1, 2024)." (2024). https://stat.gov.kz/en/industries/social-statistics/demography/publications/159623/

Portela, M., Neira, I., & Del Mar Salinas-Jiménez, M. (2013). Social Capital and Subjective Well-being in Europe: A New Approach on Social Capital. *Social Indicators Research, 114*(2), 493–511. https://doi.org/10.1007/s11205-012-0158-x

Puntscher, S., Hauser, C., Walde, J., & Tappeiner, G. (2015). The Impact of Social Capital on Subjective Well-Being: A Regional Perspective. *Journal of Happiness Studies, 16*, 1231–1246.

Ram, R. (2010). Social Capital and Happiness: Additional Cross-Country Evidence. *Journal of Happiness Studies, 11*(4), 409–418. https://doi.org/10.1007/s10902-009-9148-3

Rees, K. M., & Williams, N. W. (2017). Explaining Kazakhstani Identity: Supraethnic Identity, Ethnicity, Language, and Citizenship. *Nationalities Papers, 45*(5), 815–839. https://doi.org/10.1080/00905992.2017.1288204

Rosenfeld, M. J., & Roesler, K. (2019). Stability and Change in Predictors of Marital Dissolution in the US 1950–2015: The Rise of Family Inequality. In *Presented at the American Sociological Association Meetings in New York* [Google Scholar]. http://web.stanford.edu/~mrosenfe/Rosenfeld_and_Roesler_divorce_inequality.pdf

Ryan, R. M., & Deci, E. L. (2000). Self-determination theory and the facilitation of intrinsic motivation, social development, and well-being. *American psychologist, 55*(1), 68.

Ryff, C. D., & Morozink Boylan, J. (2016). Linking Happiness to Health: Comparisons between Hedonic and Eudaimonic Well-Being. In *Handbook of Research Methods and Applications in Happiness and Quality of Life* (pp. 53–70).

Sarbassova, G. (2015). Language and Identity in Kazakh Horse Culture/Kazak At Kültüründe Dil ve Bilinç. *Bilig (Ankara), 75*, 227.

Schulz, W., Ainley, J., Fraillon, J., Losito, B., Agrusti, G., Friedman, T., Schulz, W. et al. (2018). Introduction to the International Study of Civic and Citizenship Education. In *Becoming Citizens in a Changing World: IEA International Civic and Citizenship Education Study 2016 International Report* (pp. 1–20).

Selim, S. (2008). Life Satisfaction and Happiness in Turkey. *Social Indicators Research, 88*, 531–562.

Sen, A. (2006). Reason, Freedom and Well-Being. *Utilitas, 18*(1), 80–96.

Serikbayeva, B., & Abdulla, K. (2022). Good Governance Matters for Well-Being: The Case of Kazakhstan. *Transforming Government: People, Process and Policy, 16*(1), 140–164.

Sharipova, D., & Kudebayeva, A. (2023a). Changing Well-Being in Central Asia: Evidence from Kazakhstan and Kyrgyzstan. *Journal of Happiness Studies, 24*(3), 1233–1260.

Sharipova, D., & Kudebayeva, A. (2023b). Changing Well-Being in Central Asia: Evidence from Kazakhstan and Kyrgyzstan. *Journal of Happiness Studies, 24*(3), 1233–1260. https://doi.org/10.1007/s10902-022-00607-1

Smailov, A. A. (2000). *Natsional'nii sostav naseleniia Respbubliki Kazakhstan 1 tom: Itogi perepisi naseleniia 1999 goda v Respublike Kazakhstan* [National Composition of the Population of the Republic of Kazakhstan, Volume 1: Totals of the 1999 Census in the Republic of Kazakhstan]. Agentstvo Respubliki Kazakhstan po statistike.

Spechler, M. C. (2008). The Economies of Central Asia: A Survey. *Comparative Economic Studies, 50*(1), 30–52. https://doi.org/10.1057/ces.2008.3

Stevenson, B., & Wolfers, J. (2009). The paradox of declining female happiness. *American Economic Journal: Economic Policy, 1*(2), 190–225.

Steptoe, A., Kunz-Ebrecht, S., Owen, N., Feldman, P. J., Willemsen, G., Kirschbaum, C., & Marmot, M. (2003). Socioeconomic status and stress-related biological responses over the working day. *Biopsychosocial Science and Medicine, 65*(3), 461–470.

Suh, E., Diener, E., & Fujita, F. (1996). Events and Subjective Well-Being: Only Recent Events Matter. *Journal of Personality and Social Psychology, 70*(5), 1091.

Temirkulov, A. (2010). Kyrgyz 'Revolutions' in 2005 and 2010: Comparative Analysis of Mass Mobilization. *Nationalities Papers, 38*(5), 589–600.

Timur, D. (2006). Living Conditions, Intra-Societal Trust, and Public Concerns in Post-Socialist Turkmenistan. *Central Asia and the Caucasus, 4*(40), 122–132.

Tokhirov, A. (2023). *Income Fluctuations and Subjective Well-Being: Partially Mediating Effects of Remittances* (IOS Working Papers). https://www.econstor.eu/handle/10419/273577

Toktarov, Y., Aitymbetov, N., & Ormakhanova, Y. (2019). *Nation-Building in Kazakhstan: Kazakh and Kazakhstani Identities Controversy*. https://www.kaznu.kz/content/files/pages/folder1808/Nation-Building.pdf

Umberson, D., Williams, K., Powers, D. A., Chen, M. D., & Campbell, A. M. (2005). As Good as It Gets? A Life Course Perspective on Marital Quality. *Social Forces, 84*(1), 493–511.

United Nations. (2024). Human Development Report 2023–24. In *Human Development Reports*. United Nations. https://hdr.undp.org/content/human-development-report-2023-24

"Uzbekistan Pilot Multidimensional Poverty Index Report 2023: Poverty and Deprivation Analysis Using the Multidimensional Poverty Index (MPI) | OPHI." (2023). https://ophi.org.uk/publications/Uzbekistan-MPI-2023

Veenhoven, R. (1984). The Concept of Happiness. In R. Veenhoven (Ed.), *Conditions of Happiness* (pp. 12–38). Springer Netherlands. https://doi.org/10.1007/978-94-009-6432-7_2

Veenhoven, R. (2016). Quality of Life and Happiness: Concepts and Measures. In *Handbook of Research Methods and Applications in Happiness and Quality of Life* (pp. 309–333). Edward Elgar Publishing. https://www.elgaronline.com/abstract/edcoll/9781783471164/9781783471164.00020.xml

Waite, L., & Gallagher, M. (2001). *The Case for Marriage: Why Married People Are Happier, Healthier and Better off Financially*. Crown.

Welzel, C., & Inglehart, R. (2001). *Human Development and the "Explosion" of Democracy: Variations of Regime Change across 60 Societies*. https://www.ssoar.info/ssoar/handle/document/11513

Williams, C. C., & Horodnic, I. A. (2017). Explaining participation in the undeclared economy in Central and Eastern Europe: A demand-side approach. *Post-Communist Economies, 29*(3), 297–312.

Wilkinson, R. G., & Pickett, K. E. (2009). Income Inequality and Social Dysfunction. *Annual Review of Sociology, 35*(1), 493–511. https://doi.org/10.1146/annurev-soc-070308-115926

Winkelmann, R. (2009). Unemployment, Social Capital, and Subjective Well-Being. *Journal of Happiness Studies, 10*, 421–430.

"World Bank Open Data." (2024). *World Bank Open Data*. https://data.worldbank.org

Yamada, E., Shimizutani, S., & Murakami, E. (2022). Remittances, Household Welfare, and the COVID-19 Pandemic in Tajikistan. *Asian Development Review, 39*(2), 147–174. https://doi.org/10.1142/S0116110522500159

Yemelianova, G. M. (2013). Islam, National Identity and Politics in Contemporary Kazakhstan. *Asian Ethnicity, 15*(3), 286–301. https://doi.org/10.1080/14631369.2013.847643

MIX
Papier aus verantwortungsvollen Quellen
Paper from responsible sources
FSC® C105338

If you have any concerns about our products,
you can contact us on
ProductSafety@springernature.com

In case Publisher is established outside the EU,
the EU authorized representative is:
Springer Nature Customer Service Center GmbH
Europaplatz 3, 69115 Heidelberg, Germany

Printed by Libri Plureos GmbH
in Hamburg, Germany